SO-ANN-638

MEDITATION MUSCLE

America's New Workout for
the Mind to Increase Happiness,
Build Resiliency, and Excel
Under Pressure

By

ROBERT PIPER

Attollo Press

Photos by: Kristie Kahns

The content of this book is not intended as a substitute for the professional medical advice of your physician or other qualified health provider. The reader should regularly consult a physician in matters relating to his/her health and particularly with respect to any symptoms that may require diagnosis and treatment or medical attention. The author and publisher assume no responsibility form the result of injury or pain experienced by any of the exercises given in this book. Reliance on any information contained in this book is solely at your own risk. Never disregard professional medical advice or delay in seeking it because of something you have read in this book.

All rights reserved. No part of this book may be reproduced in any form or by any means whatsoever, electronic or mechanical or stored in a database or retrieval system. Unauthorized duplication or alteration of this book or any portion thereof without prior written permission from the publisher and author is strictly prohibited.

Published in the United States of America by Attollo Press
Copyright © 2014 Robert Piper
All rights reserved.

ISBN: 0991655508
ISBN-13: 978-0991655502

To My Father, Gerald.

CONTENTS

INTRODUCTION: HOW I STARTED MEDITATION

I was first introduced to meditation when I was 18. As a teen-ager, I was a major troublemaker and class clown. Then, at age 17, I started to suffer from panic attacks, anxiety, and digestive difficulties. This was brought on by having to deal with the day-to-day stresses that many teenagers face, such as having to do perfectly on tests in school, needing to fit in, and trying to get into the best college. Because of the overwhelming stress, I did what a lot of teenagers do when they're dealing with too much stress, I rebelled. I spent a lot of time getting in trouble, and then I had a panic attack that floored me.

These were rough days. Most of the time I spent lying in my bed only getting up to see yet another doctor, but none of them were able to help me. Towards the end of my senior year in high school, I had such debilitating symptoms that I had to withdraw from school and finish my education through homeschooling.

I was completely in the dark about my symptoms. A panic attack feels as if an intense amount of fear is overwhelming you. The only thing you can do to tame the fear is to breathe, but at the time no one had told me this. My experience with panic attacks is one of the reasons why I'm now such a huge fan of diaphragmatic breathing, Tai Chi, meditation and mindfulness, the practices that eventually were effective in helping me to regulate my breathing and calm down my nervous system.

At 18, I was told by several doctors that I might have severe panic attacks and anxiety for the rest of my life. I was not happy about such a prognosis and sought a second opinion from my family's physician, Dr. Ming-Te Lin. Dr. Ming-Te Lin is a board certified physician (allergy & immunology and pediatrics) with dual medical training (Western medicine and Traditional Chinese medicine). I was fortunate enough to have known Dr. Lin since I was 12, when my family first brought me to see him. Growing up, I'd been treated by him when I suffered from the standard seasonal allergies. After every visit, he'd give me a happy face sticker or a pencil with a yin and yang symbol on it.

Dr. Lin was one of the few doctors in our community who focused on alternative medicine when he saw patients weren't getting better by following more traditional Western methods. On his wall were hundreds of letters and pictures from families and individuals, all expressing thanks to him for healing them. I couldn't have put words on my impression of him at the time, but looking back, this man emanated a state of compassion that I'd never before experienced in my life.

Dr. Lin taught me *mindfulness,* a basic form of meditation in which the goal is to simply stay focused with your breath, bringing the mind back to the present when it wanders into thoughts. He also taught me about Tai Chi and Qigong, which are two forms of moving meditation widely used in China and Taiwan. Over the next decade, I would learn how several Eastern cultures in Tibet, China, Taiwan, and Korea have all embraced this element of compassion and mindfulness in their healthcare systems that Dr. Lin introduced me to.

But back then, as a teenager, I wasn't very motivated to meditate every day; I just didn't think it was cool. When he mentioned that it would be beneficial for me to learn to meditate more, I gave him a weird look. Dr. Lin could diagnose the skepticism in my eyes, so he referred me to a Taoist monk that taught Tai Chi and several other meditation practices, hoping that something more active would appeal to me more. I ended up studying with the Taoist monk for nine and a half years, during which time I also traveled extensively to Asia and Australia, searching out and studying with other teachers as well.

As a result of fully embracing meditation, I haven't had a severe panic attack in over 12 years! I ended up graduating from DePaul University, the largest Catholic university in America, and I used meditation throughout my time in college to manage stress. My anxiety is no longer crippling as it once was, and I now manage it with meditation, exercise, a healthy diet, and vitamins. Anxiety, when channeled in the right way, has been a positive tool for me, giving me an extra drive to succeed at things. One of the most important things it's taught me is to be resilient.

MEDITATION IN AMERICA

I love America, and I love American culture. I grew up watching MTV, listening to American music, and celebrating the 4th of July with my family and friends. I like American food, American business, and American sports. I've been using Facebook, Google, and Twitter since their inception. With all these things that make our country great, I'd like to see the practice of meditation become just as ingrained in American culture.

I'm not the only one thinking this way. Some of the most successful business personalities and celebrities in America have adopted a regular meditation practice. Top athletes in America are using meditation practices to get their minds in peak condition. The United States Marine Corps is using meditation and mindfulness to help Marines build a resilient mind, so they can better defend our country. Meditation is being used in our educational systems, from elementary school to the university level, to reduce stress and increase academic performance. It's a practice that is becoming for the mind what regular workouts are for the body—a sure-fire path to strength and resilience.

Most importantly, meditation offers us the chance to "be here now." Being present, having your attention in the present moment, means you're not wrapped up in memories of the past or to-do lists of the future. America would be a better place if we used the practice of mindful awareness to improve communication with our co-workers, spouses, or teammates on the playing field. We would live in a more cooperative, unified country if we didn't let distracting stress wear us down and hi-jack our minds and emotions.

More and more, people are adopting the practice called "mindfulness" a form of meditation that is simple and easy to learn, to gain greater voluntary control of their minds and emotions. I happen to believe that meditation is the single greatest tool for achieving and keeping a happy, strong and resilient mind. And you don't have to go into a monastery, join a cult, or change your religion to get the benefits. You can be an atheist, Buddhist, Taoist, Christian, or Jewish—it doesn't matter. I wrote this book as a workout manual for everyone, not to change or influence anyone's beliefs about his or her religion.

MY MISSION

For the past decade, I have had a one track mind for finding how meditation can make us all happier, healthier and more focused in life. I've researched every system of self-transformation and come to the conclusion that meditation is the single greatest tool to increase positive states of mind. I've traveled to several parts of Asia in search of meditation techniques. You may have heard stories of monks living in temples who are extraordinarily peaceful and happy. They exist, but my question has always been: *How do we reach that same peace and happiness without having to put in thousands of hours of meditation?*

I'm on a mission to make meditation in its many forms fun, easy and accessible for anyone to learn. I studied with some of the most authentic and traditional meditation teachers I could find. At the time of this writing, I've done well over 10,000 hours of meditation and have adapted a system for people who can't possibly do several hours of meditation in a day.

Ten to forty-five minutes a day is about all most of us can manage, and, in my system, this is enough to bring about an abundance of results. The curriculum I have developed is a synthesis of meditations used by monks in Asia for thousands of years. In my system, any type of religious attachment to the art is removed.

I see the practice of meditation as a powerful workout for the mind, similar to doing push-ups for strengthening the body or going for a jog to get your daily cardio. Meditation has got some of the brightest minds from Harvard, Yale, and Stanford backing its effectiveness as a mind-building exercise with countless scientific studies, many of which you will hear about in this book.

I also will introduce you to my method of "moving meditation" based on a combination of mindfulness, Tai Chi and Qigong. Some of the forms of meditation I will show you have been used in the health care system of China for centuries and also by warrior monks who initially developed them. Moving meditation is still in its infancy in America, both as an everyday practice and as a subject of scientific study. In this book, I will instruct you in a meditation system that I developed called *Pure Yi Systems,* or Pure Yi, for short.

I wrote this book as a basic meditation guide that you can use and share with your friends and family—regardless of your profession or other circumstances in your life. You can first skim through the book to learn how to do simple meditation techniques, or you can read it through in a one-time sitting and return to sections for further activity.

This book is about bodybuilding for the mind. In it, I show you how to build emotional muscle through training your mind for greater focus, happiness, and compassion towards others, to name just a few of the benefits. By the end of this book, you will have all you need to become a *marathon meditator*, someone who can use the techniques I offer to gain the edge in every area of your life. The meditative practices I present in this book dramatically changed my life for the better, and my hope is that they can dramatically change yours, too.

CHAPTER 1
WHY MEDITATE?

People often ask me, *Do I really need to meditate?* For me, that question is like asking, *Do I really need to eat, to sleep, or to breathe?* The answer is clearly yes, you do. I believe that having a regular meditation practice is fundamental for survival in our stressful modern life, and absolutely necessary for being healthy, happy, and powerful in life. In this book, you will learn about how science backs this truth up with a multitude of studies, most done by researchers in first-class universities. Their subjects practiced a simple form of meditation that relies on following your breath and staying present, known as *mindfulness.*

YOUR MEDITATION GOALS

You may be interested in learning more about why you should meditate and how you can get the benefits others have gotten. I can point to the many personally satisfying benefits I've gotten, but what you can get depends, of course, on your own situation.

Maybe you lost your job or are going through a difficult divorce, and now you're dealing with a great deal of stress. Maybe you are an athlete and want to sharpen your focus for a more competitive performance in your game. Or you are a new mother who feels a bit overwhelmed and wants to spend just a few minutes a day calming your mind.

Meditation is well-known as an answer to an over-stressed lifestyle, helping you to stay calm and not over-react to situations and people that you can't control. That alone is a huge benefit, impacting both your physical and emotional health. Your goals for learning to meditate may be less grand than those I've described, perhaps even mundane, like having fewer arguments with your spouse, enjoying some peace on the freeway during rush hour, or bringing down your blood pressure and getting other health issues under control. Maybe you've heard about these kinds of results and have considered learning to meditate, but you tried it and decided it was just too hard or too inconvenient for your hectic, already over-booked life.

The program you will learn about in this book combines mindfulness meditation and many forms of moving meditation to addresses all of those concerns, making it easy and convenient to become someone who knows how to keep a cool, calm center in the midst of modern stress and challenge.

MEDITATION AND THE AMERICAN CULTURE

America is one of the most resilient countries in the world. Our national DNA is composed of people who came from all over the world and took tremendous risks in getting here in spite of all odds. We are a people always looking for that

2

leading edge in all we do, which is why Americans need to adopt a practice that's been shown to increase resilience, grow happiness, and spread compassion.

Why is everyone in America not using a tool that can make a person more compassionate, resilient, kind, and happy? Half of America exercises at least three or more times a week and could as well be practicing meditation, considering the wide range of benefits.

Running marathons is *cool.* Triathlons are cool. Weight lifting is cool. Closing your eyes and bringing your attention to your breathing may not sound as cool, but I think we are overlooking a diamond in the rough that just doesn't fit with what popular culture says is cool.

Roughly 20 million Americans meditate, a fact that points to meditation being that diamond in the rough, a precious jewel caked in the mud of too many misconceptions. I'm not sure why the number of meditators isn't more like 80 million, considering how great a tool meditation is for improving our quality of life.

In my years of teaching meditation, I've concluded that one reason meditation has not been embraced by the general public is because there are so many rules associated with learning how to do it. For example, the vast majority of people think you have to sit down in a cross-legged position to meditate— you don't. Eastern cultures have been doing standing and moving forms of meditation for years. Another misconception is that you become so "blissed out" when you meditate, you can't concentrate on getting things done. But this is simply not true.

Furthermore, you don't have to listen to hippie music or burn incense to meditate. You don't even need a special meditation space with flowers and incense. You can make the world your meditation space. You can make your desk a meditation space, or the free throw line in the game, or the morning jog around the park. Anywhere you want to meditate becomes your special space.

Scientific research now validates that meditation is perhaps the greatest tool for attaining a laser-sharp mental focus, deep happiness, and a calm state of mind—things that every professional athlete and business executive should have in their arsenal. If you're a business executive or entrepreneur, the facts don't lie—you're up against a $300 billion dollar gorilla called "stress" that is smashing your profits. The facts say that American businesses are losing that amount each year because of stress-related absences or errors.

Exercise is an incredible way to reduce stress, but the combination of meditation and exercise could be the Holy Grail. A recent study reported in the *Journal of Health Psychology* done at the University of California, Davis showed how mindfulness meditation can decrease levels of the stress hormone *cortisol*. How about doing 10 minutes of meditation before you go to the gym? How about doing some meditation before you run and then leaving your iPod at home, so you can just enjoy the experience of running? How about doing it after your workout, as an extension of your warm-down?

Stress impacts your focus, and an inability to focus can cost you. If you're a professional basketball player standing at a free throw line with three seconds left in a tie game, how you manage your stress is going to impact the outcome.

Phil Jackson, perhaps one of the greatest winning basketball coaches of all time, knows this. He had all of his Los Angeles Lakers doing meditation before their game. If you're a business person, how you manage stress will be a determining factor in how well you perform. Men and women at companies such as Facebook, Aetna, Target, and General Mills are using meditation. Even members of our government are getting on the bandwagon to deal with workplace stress. Did you know that U.S. Congressman Tim Ryan practices mindfulness?

It doesn't matter who you are—an athlete or weekend warrior, top CEO or worker bee, soccer mom or career woman—every day you are encountering hundreds of stressors and fears that stop you from achieving what you want in life. Meditation helps you to recognize this negative process and build a buffer zone to protect you from it, so you don't have to waste your precious energy by reacting to everyday events with toxic emotions. Meditation also makes you happier, and, when you are happier, your family life and work life go smoother and are more enjoyable.

Reasons to Meditate

Here are just a few of the many reasons why I believe meditation should become ingrained in our American culture as something we all do:

1. *Meditation can make you happier by giving you access to more positive emotions.* The practice helps you to cultivate more positive states of mind, and, if you're happy, you will do better in every area of your life. Emotions are contagious, and, when you're happy, you spread that feeling to everyone around you. A study done by the University of Wisconsin-Madison suggested mindfulness meditation increases positive emotions in the brain.
2. *Meditation strengthens the brain.* Studies done at UCLA suggest that meditation actually strengthens the brain in a good way. The brain is just like a muscle you work out at your gym: If you do meditation every day, it's going to positively influence your life.
3. *Meditation can help you focus at work.* Our hectic, technology-filled lifestyle is taking all of our attention. We are all constantly checking emails, Facebook updates, and Twitter feeds. A study done at the Information School at the University of Washington suggests that meditation may make you more focused at work.
4. *Meditation may lower anxiety and depression levels.* A recent study published in the *Journal of the American Medical Association Internal Medicine* done at Johns Hopkins University suggested that 8 weeks of doing mindfulness meditation could lower anxiety and depression up to 38%,

roughly similar to what someone would experience if they took anti-depressant medication.

5. *Meditation can make you a more compassionate person.* Meditation helps you to calm down by centering on your breathing and the sensations in your body. It also helps you recognize positive emotions within your own body and use those emotions to act more compassionately toward others. A new study by Northeastern University and Harvard University researchers showed that people who meditated were kinder to others after meditating than those who did not meditate.

6. *Meditation might help you lose weight.* Researchers at the University of California, San Francisco conducted a study that suggests meditation could aid in weight loss. Mindfulness is a way to pay attention to all the sensations you're experiencing. When you are mindful while eating, you become more conscious of what you are putting in your mouth and are less likely to overeat.

7. *Meditation may relieve stress.* A study in the *Journal of Health Psychology* done at the University of California, Davis showed that mindfulness decreased levels of the stress hormone cortisol. Decreased stress is something everyone in American could use, considering stress has literally become an epidemic in our country.

8. *Meditation might help you do better in school.* A new study reported in the journal *Mindfulness* done at George Mason University and the University of Illinois showed that meditation improved the test scores of students in a psychology class. Some of the students meditated before the lecture, and another group did not. After the lecture, those who meditated did better on an exam. Want your kids to do better in class? Why not teach them how to meditate?

9. *Meditation might help American troops.* A number of programs are working with our troops to give them the tools of meditation to better their quality of life. Organizations like Project Welcome Home Troops, the Mind Fitness

Training Institute, and the Samueli Institute are all using meditation with the military. A study done at the University of California, San Diego School of Medicine and Naval Health Research Center suggested that meditation may help Marines prepare and recover faster from stressful events in combat-related situations.

10. ***Meditation may protect you against colds.*** A study done at the University of Wisconsin-Madison showed that people who practiced mindfulness meditation or engaged in physical exercise suffered less from colds than those who did neither.

Cheers to meditation, America's new push-up exercise for the brain! With all the scientific evidence coming in over the years, meditation is now becoming a practice that anyone from any walk of life can embrace. You don't have to practice any religion or have any set of beliefs to use this incredible tool for the brain. All you need to have is the commitment to take on a regular practice ... and breathe!

What Meditation Muscle is *NOT*:

1. Something that turns you into a sissy.
2. A cult.
3. An activity that requires a $300 meditation pillow imported from the Himalayas.
4. Having to burn incense, chant, and sit cross-legged for hours.
5. Being "spaced out" all day, unable to concentrate.
6. Something that dampens your ambitions or goals.
7. Un-American.
8. A religion.
9. Too difficult to learn.
10. Something people will think you are weird for doing.

CHAPTER 2

BUILD YOUR BRAIN
WITH MEDITATION

Meditation is for the champions out there who want not only to improve their own life, but also to contribute to the lives of others—champions who want to change the world for the better. The first goal of being a champion is to build a resilient mind that can pierce through any obstacle you may be facing. It doesn't matter if you're starting a charity or a business, or if you're coaching a football team. You need a strong mind, and that starts with building your brain through meditation.

Each and every one of us wants to be happy. This is what we wake up in the morning for—the possibility of a day filled with satisfaction and well-being. Most of us want to impact the world and make it a better place. It doesn't matter if you're a janitor, businessperson, professional athlete, or professor. In order to make a difference, you have to take care of your inner self first. We all have access to cultivating positive states of mind that enable us to plow through any setback we face.

Your natural state is pure undivided happiness, with no limitations. You need to use your mind to take back your concentration, so you are not buffeted by negative emotions that can run amok and take you off your goals in life. Meditation is about honing your attention and breaking down the limits you see in your life, so you can live a life with less stress and more happiness, and be better able to achieve your goals.

The techniques I offer in this book are going help you side step the blocks within your own mind, using a tool that has been around for over 2,500 years—*meditation.*

THE BULL IN THE CHINA SHOP—AKA YOUR MIND

How many times have you laid in your bed at night, trying to sleep when it feels as though an out-of-control locomotive is running through your head? You toss and turn, get out of bed to get a glass water, trying every way possible to fall back asleep only to glimpse the clock and realize it's time to go to work. As you get up to prepare breakfast, you realize you haven't slept much during the night. You now have a thousand different thoughts and a to-do list running through your mind. Finish the report by Friday, take the kids to soccer practice on Thursday, pick up your dry cleaning, etc. You're already exhausted and the day hasn't yet begun.

How many times have you sat at work, frustrated because you just have too much on your plate? You've had several sleepless nights, and you have to answer hundreds of emails. Anxiety starts to take hold, a condition estimated to affect 40 million people in America.

These emotions that you are facing are a result of the stress that has hijacked your mind. In some reports, over 79% of people say they experience stress as a common, everyday occurrence. Stress is the bubonic plague of our age, as it impacts every area of our health from high blood pressure, heart attacks, diabetes, lower immune function, depression, and anxiety. And the list goes on and on. Many of those conditions are the result of a mind that is unable to focus and become calm in the midst of the eroding effects of constant stress and negative emotions, such as anger, fear, and hopelessness.

Meditation is about becoming a champion of your own mind and training it to behave on your terms. You can train it as you do any muscle, building it to become stronger and more focused through a simple practice you regularly repeat.

BUILDING MENTAL MUSCLE

In this book, I show you how to do push-ups for your brain. By doing the various focusing exercises I will teach you, you will have access to a greater degree of voluntary control over your mind. When you build mental muscle, you have:

1. More awareness of emotions in your body.
2. The ability to manage your emotions and not be at their whim.
3. The ability to channel your emotions toward a specific goal.
4. Compassion and empathy towards others.
5. Reduced stress.
6. Better communication skills.

ATTENTION: YOUR MOST IMPORTANT MENTAL MUSCLE

Your attention—what you focus on—is the most important mental capability you have in life and so is an important "muscle" to build. How you direct your attention is how you shape the quality of your life. Attention can make or break a relationship with your spouse, business partner, teammate, teacher, or client. If you use your attention to focus on the negative aspects of your life, you will have negative experiences; if you focus on the positive, that is what you will experience.

By learning to meditate, you can return to that original state of pure happiness that you were born with. In order to do that, you need to focus on strengthening your meditation muscle to gain the ability to stand apart from your own distracting thoughts and emotions. Then you will be able to guide your attention in the direction you would like it to go. If you are a parent, you can use your meditation muscle to become more focused in your communication with your children. If you're an athlete, you can use your attention to improve your game, so you spend more time in "the zone," not only enjoying the experience but achieving the results you desire.

You can use your "meditation muscle" to get in touch with emotions in your body, enabling you to communicate better with others. You can feel certain emotions more clearly and be able to recognize others' feelings more easily. You become more open to giving to others and more able to improve relationships with co-workers, teammates, and your spouse.

One of the easiest ways to develop this quality is to simply close your eyes and recognize that it is already within you. Your attention is the driving force in your life. In order to strengthen your attention, you must first get control of your own mind. With so many distractions in our modern lives, our attention is scattered all over the place. Some people have three to five electronic devices activated and in use at any one time. They may be typing an e-mail while surfing the Internet and also watching TV. We all do this at times, but do you need to do it all day long? *That* is a recipe for a distracted mind.

A recent Internet trends report by Kleiner Perkins Caufield & Byers suggested that the average person checks his or her smartphone 150 times a day. Can you imagine what that is doing to your brain's capacity for attention? You want to become more conscious of what you are doing on a day-to-day basis with your attention. Many worry that cell phones have become a major obstacle to developing social skills needed in life. People have their eyes glued to their smartphone when their attention could be more directed to talking face-to-face with another person, having a more human interaction. You can make the choice to take your attention back to the present moment and focus it on the people with whom you are communicating.

Think of your attention as the most important thing you have to help you become conscious of areas of your life you want to improve. For example, your attention, whether focused or unfocused, actually has a massive influence on the people in your life with whom you communicate. Imagine a father who comes home after work: As soon as he walks in the door, his kids greet him, but Dad is stuck to his smartphone, reading his emails, and fails to make any meaningful contact. This is a fairly common scenario in America today. Children need communication and empathy to properly grow into adults, and, when it is lacking, it can cause negative effects later on in life.

The best way to begin to focus and strengthen your attention is to learn a simple breathing technique, as described below:

BREATHING FROM THE BELLY (DIAPHRAGMATIC BREATHING)

1. Take a seat on your couch, chair, or wherever you have a place to sit in your home or office. Don't lie down for this particular exercise. Try to sit with an erect spine—it doesn't have to be perfect posture, just a straight back.
2. Close your eyes and bring your awareness to the area of your belly. Try to feel your rib cage and tail bone.
3. Now bring your attention to your breathing. As you breathe in and out, focus on all the sensations going on in your body, such as your heart beating, your ribs expanding and contracting, your belly area rising and falling.

4. Expect your mind to wander, because that's what the mind does. When it does, bring your attention back to your breathing and bodily sensations. Don't criticize yourself; don't try to wrestle with your thoughts or stop them in any way. Simply return your attention to your breathing and your body every time you become aware that you have lost your focus.
5. After just the right amount of focused attention, a door may open and you will experience being calm, collected, and sharply aware. Emotions can come up, but let them do what they do, as if you are watching the surface of an ocean: sometimes, there are waves, and sometimes, it is smooth.
6. Now bring all of your awareness back and open your eyes.

The main goal of this meditation is to focus on your breathing and your body. You want to try and get a calm, smooth rhythm down when in meditation. Again, you are building a muscle of attention, and each day you will make it become stronger. After a while, you will be able to side-step your thoughts and not be concerned with them. Most important, this phenomenon of inner calmness and meta-attention will show up in your life as you go about your daily activities. You will notice that you are able to direct your attention more and more easily, becoming less distracted and more focused in all you do.

Don't be surprised if, at the end of a few minutes of this meditation, you open your eyes and have an "Aha" moment. Something becomes crystal clear that was bothering you or causing some difficulty in your life. At those times, you achieve the deepest levels of a calm state of happiness and focus.

At other times, you will have disturbing thoughts or emotions during your focused breathing. But an important aspect of this practice is not judging yourself or your experience. Treat all the negative emotions as water under the bridge; you are aware of them but they are not the sturdy Golden Gate Bridge that you are, rather just the water running underneath it. The value of observing your emotions and letting them go is that you become conscious of negative thoughts that are impacting your life—becoming mindfully aware of them, so you can change them rather than have them run you unconsciously.

CHANGING YOUR PHYSICAL BRAIN

Meditation works on actual physical areas of your brain, as shown by the last two decades of brain research using advanced technology. A key structure for understanding this is the foremost section of your brain, an area known as the *frontal lobe*. The frontal lobe is the executive branch of your brain, and it helps you to make better decisions not only in business, but also in everyday life. By becoming conscious of your attention and learning to train it through practicing meditation, you are building this area up, directly influencing it for the better.

A study done at UCLA showed that, just by doing a few weeks of meditation, lasting changes occur, showing actual physical alterations in the brain. Similar to doing push-ups to strengthen your upper body, doing meditation strengthens your frontal lobe. On the other hand, by not using your attention correctly, you are also altering your brain in detrimental ways. This is because your brain has the quality of *neuroplasticity*, the ability to be formed and shaped by your experience and thoughts. Because of this, it's extremely important to focus on what you want, because that is what your brain will then become "wired" to give you as it shifts neural networks in response to your thinking.

AMYGDALA: FIGHT OR FLIGHT RESPONSE

Let's look a little closer at your brain structures. Your *amygdala* is the fear center of your brain, a tiny peanut-sized structure in the middle of your brain that packs an immensely powerful punch. It was designed to keep the human species alive over millions of years of evolution. The amygdala is where you first sense danger and are therefore able to respond quickly, either standing to *fight* or *fleeing* for safety— the "fight-or-flight" response. It's a safety mechanism in your brain, alerting you to danger, but it can go on overload, which is why the military and law enforcement are particularly interested in learning how to control it. Soldiers and police officers are always looking for ways to tame the amygdala, so it doesn't hijack the brain and cause a chronic fear reaction, impeding the ability to act in an emergency.

Our emotions can spread like a fire, thanks to our trigger-happy reptilian brain. If a fire starts in one area of the house, you have to put it out, or it will spread to the other areas. Likewise, when you recognize a harmful emotion in your life, you want to be able to let it go. The goal is to not to over-react when you experience a negative emotion. Every time you choose *not* to yell at your co-worker, you are altering your prefrontal lobe. Emotions are a driving force of life, guiding you to achieve your goals, motivating you, and allowing you to fall in love with a significant partner.

One of the most powerful ways meditation can be used is to help people recognize negative emotions, such as anger, in their body. I think the simple technique of mindfulness practice should be taught in every jail in the world. Imagine if convicted felons took classes that helped them recognize and deal with their negative emotions. Even better, what if children were taught about their brain and emotions, and how to mindfully manage their emotions from an early age? What if children were taught how to turn anger towards another human being into compassion? Could you imagine how much safer and more peaceful this world we live in would be?

ANGER MINDFULNESS TECHNIQUE

When you get angry, your fight-or-flight reaction is coming from your old brain, moving away from the frontal lobes (where you can choose) and toward an area where your more animal instincts lie—the amygdala and other emotional centers. Here is a simple technique to reverse that direction:

1. When you get angry, first recognize the emotion. Name it by saying, *I'm angry*. Recognize that it is not the most resourceful emotion you can have in the situation.
2. Take deep breaths, in through the nose, out through the mouth. It's best to take at least 4 or 5 deep breaths.
3. After controlling your breathing by focusing your attention, do something different. Go mow the lawn, clean your kitchen, or play some calming music. Continue to breathe consciously as any anger continues to surface.

EMOTIONS AND FOCUS

Focus is the main objective when performing at your best, because, by focusing clearly, you can open all kinds of options in your life. However, in order to focus on the outer properly, you have to first turn inward to notice all the feelings and sensations in your body. When you develop focus, you are working the more evolved area of your brain called the prefrontal cortex. When this area is lit up on scan, it shows you rely less on primitive emotions like fear, anger, aggression, etc.

Focusing on all the emotions in your body gives you the access to use these emotions in life. In reality, emotions are one of the major driving forces behind our lives. If you are confident, you will make confident decisions in life. If you are motivated, you will take motivated actions. Rather than focusing on your doubts and worries, you can shift your focus to resourceful emotions. With this ability, you can bring about massive changes in your life for the better. If you put a reminder note on your wall that says just one word, *FOCUS*, and you incorporate that into your life, you would see changes happening every day.

Confidence is an emotional state that many of us want, and you can get confidence through training your focus. People who appear more confident have an easier time persuading people and becoming successful. The easiest way to become more confident is to gain access to the emotions inside you that make you more confident, such as peace and happiness. By being mindful and practicing meditation, you can train yourself to experience confidence more often.

CONFIDENCE VISUALIZATION MEDITATION

1. Close your eyes, breathe, and visualize a time in your life when you felt totally confident. It could be when you won a game, closed a big business deal, or spoke in front of a group of parents at your child's school.
2. Now focus on how great that feeling was. Let that feeling flood your body and feel all of the other emotions that come along with it.
3. Now open your eyes. By doing this simple visualization, you establish an anchor to come back to whenever you lack confidence. Repeat it often.

Remember, your brain is like a muscle, and, every time you bring an emotion to the surface, you're strengthening your brain to experience that feeling more often. You are re-wiring your brain for more positive emotions, building mental muscle every time you practice these simple forms of meditation.

CHAPTER 3
TAKE CONTROL OF YOUR MIND

Here's a shocking statistic: According to the federal government's Centers for Disease Control and Prevention, it's estimated that *only* 17% of adults in America are considered to have optimal mental health. By 2020, depression is predicted to be the second-leading cause of disability throughout the entire world (ischemic heart disease is currently number one). In the past two decades, the use of anti-depressant drugs prescribed by doctors to treat depression and anxiety has risen 400%!

But it's not only adults in our society who are suffering from mental health issues. According to a recent study in the *Journal of the American Academy of Child and Adolescent Psychiatry,* about 11% of children ages 4 to 17 years of age have been diagnosed with *attention deficit hyperactivity disorder* (ADHD).

Emotional well-being can be attributed to a variety of influences, including environmental, dietary, and stress-related. However, regardless of the cause, there's no denying that Americans of all ages are in the midst of an epidemic of unhappiness.

WHAT HAPPENED TO HAPPINESS?

For thousands of years, we human beings have derived happiness from our relationships, whether romantic, friendship, familial or broader forms of community. This is a huge contrast to modern times. Back then, we didn't spend our entire life accumulating material objects. We didn't spend our entire life staring at a smartphone or trying to get a better car than our neighbor. We didn't look at magazine covers and try to emulate unattainable body styles by working out for thousands of hours and radically changing our eating habits.

Can we be happy today? Yes, but it takes shifting our priorities and honing our attention. Happiness starts with choosing to not work so many hours a week that you don't make it home to spend time with your spouse and children. Happiness starts with mindfully paying attention to the person you are speaking with and not focusing on your smartphone. Happiness starts with letting the driver on the freeway merge into your lane during bumper-to-bumper, rush hour traffic. Happiness starts with turning off your laptop when you're speaking with your child. Happiness starts with realizing that you are perfect the way you are and don't need to fix or change yourself to match some societal ideal.

Happiness is about saying something nice to a stranger or helping someone out at a time of need. Growing up, we're told not to talk to strangers. I think we would live in a happier place if we did talk to strangers. You don't have to be Mother Theresa, Gandhi, or Martin Luther King Jr. to help a stranger. If you see someone in the parking lot of a convenient store struggling to lift a box into a car, why not ask, *Can I help you with that?*

Let me give you some advice on this: Throw your first thought away. Most people's first thought is something like, *I'm too busy, I'll be late,* or *they don't really need my help.* But that is only the first thought. The practice of mindfulness meditation helps you to observe your first thoughts and recognize selfish thoughts that pop into your mind to go unexamined, preventing you from helping another person. By becoming more mindful of your thinking, you can choose how you respond to others, not just have knee-jerk reactions with your first thought. With mindfulness, you can positively influence people around you, and you'll be happier when you do.

You encounter people everyday who can do absolutely nothing for you—there is nothing to be gained by talking with them. But try talking to them anyway! Why? Because they might be having a terrible day and you could cheer them up. If you cheer them up, they'll go home to their spouse or children in a happier mood. You set in motion a domino effect, and you never know how many lives are affected by just you talking to one "stranger."

We can't forget though, that mindful awareness is a skill that has to be honed every day. As suggested, positive thinking literally has a massive impact on your health, so it's always good to use positive self-talk throughout the day.

Re-wire Your Brain

Want to be happier? Focus on happiness. Want to be more compassionate? Focus on compassion. The science is in on this one. Through a capacity of the brain known as *neuroplasticity*, you can actually use your attention to re-wire your own brain and, as a result, have more positive states and outcomes.

Neurons that fire together, wire together is a catchy phrase that neuroscientists use to summarize Hebb's Law in pointing to another example of neuroplasticity. Anything you focus on—a thought, a feeling, a memory—causes firing of your brain's neural networks—those multitudes of tiny pathways made up of associated brain cells. If you return your attention over and over again to one thought or feeling, those networks become linked and strengthened, eventually hard-wiring into your brain. If you focus on calm, happy, and serene states of mind, you are training your brain to "hold" that focus—to become tame.

Visualization—holding a picture in your mind—while meditating can be an incredible tool for athletes, thanks to the brain's neuroplasticity. If you are working out frequently and want to better your form in the gym when lifting weights, why not visualize yourself using the perfect form beforehand? Some of the greatest bodybuilders in America have recommended that weight lifters should be 100% focused while lifting weights. When you lift, you want to be able to use every muscle fiber dedicated to lifting weights. Visualizing and focusing on your muscles doing just that, over and over again, can re-wire your brain and make it easier to lift more and more weight. This is an example of exercising not only your body, but your brain as well!

For thousands of years, the Samurai warriors of Japan, known for their battle prowess, used meditation to help them focus, not only for martial arts, but for farming, archery, making tools—almost everything they needed to do in life. The Samurai were aware that fear is the opposite of the calm state of a meditative focus and can be a major toxic substance in the mind.

MOVING AWAY FROM FEAR

Fear is a good thing when it stops you from walking across a busy street and getting run over by a car. However, too much of it can cause a whole host of problems. For one, fear can put major limits on how much success you have in life. Fear can step in when you think you deserve a raise and stops you from asking for one because you are afraid of what your boss might say.

Fear creeps into every area of life. All great leaders have been challenged by fear—no one escapes it. For thousands of years, in a variety of cultures and locations, people have managed their fear through the simple practice of mindful awareness. The steps are clear: Learn to recognize a fear, study it, befriend it, and you can conquer it in any situation. You can surmount any obstacle that fear throws at you.

The only difference between an amateur and a pro is that a pro has failed more times consecutively than an amateur, and so has learned to manage fear. No one ever does away with fear completely; it's always lurking in the background, patiently stalking like a lion and ready to pounce on its prey.

One of the most powerful tools you can use to influence every area of your life is to mindfully manage your fear. That means being still enough within your own mind to recognize when you are coming from a fear and then not reacting in ways that stop you from accomplishing your goals. Every high-performance athlete mindfully manages fear. Mindfulness is the tool that could help you become more conscious of fear in your everyday life.

Here are some tips for managing fear mindfully as it arises to stop you in whatever you are up to:

1. When you first become aware of a strong fear response, bring your attention to your breathing. Stay with your breath until the fear weakens and you can choose how to act.
2. Become a witness of your fear, rather than the object of it. What does it feel like in your body? How does it affect your breathing, your heart beat? Watch it closely with mindful awareness.
3. Recognize that fear is only a temporary feeling; it will pass as you befriend it.
4. Use mindful awareness every day to recognize your fears and then move past them. You can conquer your fears little by little by using mindful awareness.

Fear can be an overwhelmingly powerful emotion and not always easy to manage, but it can be done. Some days you have anxiety, and some days you don't. But the goal is to separate from the feeling—become the witness rather than the victim—and push through it. If you aren't able to separate yourself from your fear, it will just keep coming at you and eventually take over to run your life. This may not necessarily be dramatic; it can happen in quiet ways you might not even notice. But background fear gives a quality of life that is less than what you could be having without the fear permeating everything you do.

BREAKING DOWN MENTAL BARRIERS

Success in any area of life is about breaking down the mental barriers that hold you back from getting what you really want. And those mental barriers are mostly fear-based. We are indoctrinated from birth to cling to mental models that tell us how to interpret the world and then react to our surroundings through those mental models. But these models can be broken, and new, greater advancements, both personal and professional, can be achieved.

Steve Jobs came up with the revolutionary new model of personal computing in the home. Models are malleable, and they can be changed and manipulated to create something new. They are not set in stone. We all have mental models for how we view the world, and these models can become rigid and run your life, especially when they relate to self-concept. *I'm not good enough, I'm too old, I'm too fat* are all just mental models, not reality. If we accept certain mental models blindly, without observing them within ourselves, they become habits that run our lives. Then, even though you may become successful, you are never really happy.

Why don't we Westerners look within, as do people in the East, for the happiness and purpose we so desperately want? Our society is so conditioned by the media to seek solutions outside ourselves that most of us never even begin the journey inward for finding lasting happiness. Instead, we find things to dull the pain and boredom—such as drugs, alcohol and sex—and fill the void of what is missing. But what if people knew that the emptiness they feel within can be filled by turning inward to find their truth, and not by the pain-numbing mask of an external substance?

It is from the inner view you get from meditation that you begin to recognize this simple truth: *all your answers lie within.* When you discover this for yourself, through simply watching your thoughts and feelings, you develop the capacity to transcend any limitation that is brought upon you. You can become free of fear and all mental models that stop you.

When practicing meditation, you come to recognize that you are not your thoughts. Thousands of random thoughts pass through your mind every minute, all coming from your parents, peer groups, what somebody said to you randomly, movies you've watched, lyrics to songs you've heard, and memories of fearful experiences.

These thoughts are not you! You don't have to let them impact and eventually control your life. All of us have thoughts that limit us, but that doesn't mean you have to let them control you. Real victory in life comes from not letting your life run you. The opponent you face and must conquer is inside of you, not outside of you.

Want to start a company? Become an actor? Start a non-for-profit? What's stopping you? Only your fearful thoughts—nothing else. Learn to distinguish between the two—what is your thoughts and what is real—because, when the two become collapsed into one, you become confused and cannot tell them apart. You think your fearful thoughts are your truth when they are not. Every day, you must train like a warrior to overcome fearful thoughts from controlling you, working hard to observe your thoughts from a distance and not identifying with them.

MEDITATION: YOU ARE NOT YOUR THOUGHTS

One of the biggest fears people have is the fear of failure. Everybody hates failing, but you have to be able to become friends with failure. Why? Because if you are intending to do anything worth doing, one thing is for sure: you are going to face failure on the way there.

Imagine that you are alone in a boat the middle of a lake, and, overhead, a flock of geese are flying by. Your thoughts are like those geese, noisily distracting you from the quiet beauty of the still lake. Move away from focusing on the geese. No matter how loud they honk and make their raucous geese noises, keep focusing on the beauty all around you, surrounded by the still waters of the lake.

Follow these steps:

1. Focus on the image of the lake and geese as described above.
2. Breathe in from your nose, deeply into your belly (diaphragmatic breathing).
3. Breathe out your nose (or mouth). Keep your focus on the lake image and your breathing.
4. When thoughts intrude, just relax and breathe deeper, returning to the simple image of the still, calm lake.

This takes practice, but every day you can get better and better at staying focused in your own peaceful state. By practicing every day, you are building a mental muscle, just as you would build up your biceps from repeated workouts. Only practicing meditation is a workout for your mind, and the end result is a calmer, more peaceful and more capable you.

MAKE FAILURE YOUR FRIEND: RESILIENCE

Every successful person in this world has had to deal with some form of failure. Name a successful person you know, and you will find several instance where he or she failed before overcoming the obstacle. Each time, these people came back stronger, building the quality of resilience.

According to the Merriam-Webster dictionary, the word *resilience* points to a choice that you make to not quit. Resilience has nothing to do with the circumstances in your life, although, after repeated failure, you may submit and see yourself as a powerless victim. But being resilient means you bounce back and make a choice to press on. Meditation is a tool that can help you to press on and not give up in the face of even the most seemingly insurmountable obstacles. No matter what you do for a living or want to accomplish in your life, you must become resilient if you are to succeed.

There is nothing worse than when your brain hijacks your thoughts and feelings. One thought, feeling, or experience can send you into a downward spiral. The reality is that no matter what happens to you, you are not the negative feelings your brain is having. Your true self is the observer to these negative feelings and thoughts that are occurring in your brain. And because you are the observer, you have the ability to approach your thoughts and feelings in a loving and compassionate way.

After a catastrophic loss, you will experience intense emotions. One thing I can attest to is that the mind is one of the most resilient tools on the planet; it's capable of some of the most extraordinary acts. Always remember this, and you will find strength in anything you do.

Some professional athletes experience absolutely devastating defeats which are hard to bounce back from. There are countless stories of CEOs losing their entire company and then using their focus to bounce back. What you focus on, you become; if you focus on feeling terrible, you'll feel terrible. If you focus on compassion, you'll act more compassionate towards others.

IMPORTANCE OF FOCUS

What you focus on is as important as the food you put in your mouth. If you put bad food in your mouth, it will eventually have a massive impact on your health. The same is true of what you are focusing on; if you focus on the bad things in life, you'll be letting those things in.

Mindfulness in the moment helps you to hone in on a calm, collected focus, and mindfulness of the breath brings you back to this state if you veer off it. If you are writing, just write! Don't have 12 windows open on your browser and your smartphone next to you playing music in your ear. You would be amazed at how many people go through their day with multiple devices playing in the background. Over-stimulation by technology has been linked to anxiety and depression.

Always remember, if you don't experience the success, peace, and fulfillment you want, that you must work on your focus to bring it about. Remember, the brain exhibits neuroplasticity and that *neurons that fire together, wire together*. This means that whatever feeling or thought you repeat reinforces your brain's neural networks to become hardwired —it doesn't matter if it's negative or positive.

So what can you do to break up this negative loop? Change your focus! You can change your focus to something else, like reading a book, going for a run, or watching a movie. The goal here is to intentionally and fully shift your focus. Your "meditation muscle" is a tool that will help you do this.

ACTIVITY: WHERE IS YOUR FOCUS?

List four things you focus on that you *don't* want in your life.

1.
2.
3.
4.

List four ways you could change your focus to what you *do* want in your life.

1.
2.
3.
4.

CULTIVATE RESILIENCE

You can shift your focus from failure to success by cultivating the quality of resilience. In Latin, *resili (ēns)* means "to spring back," to rebound. It's a brilliant feeling, one that can cause a human being to change the world.

Pablo Picasso was someone who did just that. If you were to walk into an art museum and view an original painting by Picasso, you'd see an artistic genius who was sick and tired of the norms installed by previous generations of artists. He painted the way he felt, not the way he was taught to paint; he painted with emotions that came from his ability to be resilient in life.

Picasso's work from his Blue Period is a showcase of resiliency. The Blue Period was said to have taken place during the artist's experience with severe bouts of depression due to his friend, Carlos Casagemas, committing suicide. He wasn't painting to become rich because, at the time, no one was interested in the type of painting he did. Picasso is quoted as saying, "I started painting in blue when I learned of Casagemas' death." It was the great painter's way of rebounding from his tragic loss.

After his Blue Period, Picasso went on to produce some of the most creative and inspiring pieces of art ever made. Today almost every child who goes to an art class is shown paintings from Picasso's Blue Period as an example of magnificent art.

Elisabeth Kübler-Ross spoke about resilience when she said, "The most beautiful people we have known are those who have known defeat, known suffering, known struggle, known loss, and have found their way out of the depths. These persons have an appreciation, a sensitivity, and an understanding of life that fills them with compassion, gentleness, and a deep loving concern. Beautiful people do not just happen."

Abraham Lincoln suffered with severe depression during his life, and while, historians will argue that he freed the slaves for political reasons only, I believe he did it for another reason. He freed the slaves because he suffered immensely his entire life with severe depression, and he saw the same suffering in the slaves.

Lincoln wrote a few times to his friend Joshua Speed explaining his battle with depression and thoughts of suicide. Through his own suffering, he was able to build compassion towards the suffering of others. His depression made him shift his focus to do something incredible—something that changed the world. In 1854, in his Peoria Speech about the Kansas Slavery Act, Lincoln said, "I hate it because of the monstrous injustice of slavery itself. I hate it because it deprives our Republican example of its just influence in the world."

Mahatma Gandhi spent 21 years in South Africa where he built up the resiliency and tenacity to eventually change the world. During that time, Gandhi was thrown off a train in Pietermaritzburg, South Africa, because he was of a different color than the other passengers. This aggravated him, and he stood up and protested. Because of his protest, he was allowed to sit in first class the next day. One day, however, he was beaten because he refused to give up his seat to a European passenger. He encountered numerous injustices while in South Africa; in one instance, he was asked to take his turban off, and he refused.

It was in South Africa that Gandhi cultivated the resiliency that enabled him to do the impossible, which was to take on the British Empire in his own country, India. At the time, the British military ruled India; they were proud and often dressed as if they were prestigious gentlemen. But Gandhi one-upped them because he exhibited the qualities of a true gentleman, more so than they could ever hope to be. The British ordered Indian people to buy British products only, so Gandhi started to make his own clothing with yarn and a wheel. He changed the paradigm of what it means to be a leader, and was famous for saying, "A coward is incapable of exhibiting love; it is the prerogative of the brave."

Martin Luther King Jr. was probably one of the most resilient human beings in history. He was a clergyman, activist, and leader of the African-American Civil Rights Movement. He was greatly influenced by Gandhi to use nonviolent methods of resistance to change the political landscape of America. Through his resiliency and charisma, Dr. King changed the lives of millions of people. On August 28, 1963, in a speech at the Lincoln Memorial in Washington, DC, he said, "I have a dream that one day this nation will rise up and live out the true meaning of its creed: *We hold these truths to be self-evident: that all men are created equal.*"

Fleeing Tibet decades ago, the Dalai Lama had everything including his entire country stripped from him. It was a demonstration of true resiliency that, instead of hating the Chinese Government, he offered kindness and compassion to them.

Steve Jobs, arguably one of the most resilient entrepreneurs who ever lived, worked tirelessly to build up Apple, a company that he started in his garage with Steve Wozniak. Jobs had dedicated almost his entire life to building Apple, only to be completely stripped of any ownership of the company. The board of directors ended up kicking him out in 1985. He then went on to build two successful companies—NeXT Computer and Pixar. In 1997, he returned to Apple and put the company back on the map as one of the most innovative companies in the world, which it is today.

BECOME INSPIRED

They say a cat has nine lives—but I say a human being with a soul on fire has a thousand lives. In your own life, you may fail hard, get hurt hard—but it will make you come back stronger. Look to cultivate this beautiful resilient attitude in everything you do, and you will amass strength that you never thought possible. There are so many stories in history of human beings who surmounted almost impossible circumstances to go on to change the world.

Regardless of what you're going through in your life, you can always find someone who has overcome huge obstacles and can inspire you. Everyone has to face hardships, even though you may think you are the only one going through a particular event. Here are some examples that inspire me:

The actor Dwayne Johnson, also known as the "The Rock," named his company 7 Bucks Entertainment because in 1995 he had exactly seven bucks in his pocket and wanted to change his circumstances. Fast forward to now, Dwayne Johnson is one of the most successful actors and former World Wrestling Entertainment stars in the world.

Sylvester Stallone, before the success of the movie *Rocky*, was so broke he sold his dog for $50. After he sold the script for *Rocky*, he went to purchase back his dog, but the guy he sold it to wouldn't sell the dog back. Stallone finally got the dog back for $3,000!

Ted Turner, who founded CNN and made massive contributions to television, took over his father's company at age 24, right after his father committed suicide. Some of the members in the company tried to kick him out, but he wouldn't quit and instead built the broadcasting empire we know today.

TEACHING CHILDREN TO CHANGE THEIR BRAINS

Meditation can help you to focus and become resilient in the face of anything that tries to stop you from being a success in the world. Even school children can learn to change their brains, and, when they do, we can expect a future generation empowered to change the world in unprecedented ways.

The actress Goldie Hawn has put together a team of some of the leading neuroscientist and educators in the world to formulate a school curriculum called MindUp that teaches children how to use their brains. Our brain is capable of producing absolutely astonishing things. It can produce the next scientific discovery, create music never heard before, and even change the world—if used correctly.

The ability to recognize emotions is probably the single most important tool children can learn. Self-awareness and self-regulation are tools that the MindUp program is teaching children to utilize. MindUp teaches children how to recognize positive emotions in their brains such as kindness, happiness, and empathy.

Think about how many problems in the world could be solved if children were taught from a young age how to recognize emotions, such as aggression, and then turn those negative emotions into kindness.

Scientists know that an area of the brain's frontal lobe called the *pre-frontal cortex* doesn't fully develop until around the age of 25. The pre-frontal cortex is in charge of planning, reasoning, and impulse control. Mindfulness meditation practice may be able to strengthen this area of the brain. Thus, many children become aggressive and hyperactive because they don't yet know how to properly manage their emotions and control their impulses.

The MindUp program is looking to give children mindful education tools to bring emotional balance and well-being into their lives. One of the activities taught is called the "amygdala shake-up," referring to the part of the brain where emotions hijack behavior. This activity teaches students to be patient—something I wish was taught when I was in school. The teacher holds up a Coke bottle filled with sand and glitter, then shakes it up to show students what happens when we get angry. The teacher then puts the bottle down so the sand and glitter can settle—very slowly in the water. This gives the students a visual demonstration of how long it takes for the amygdala to calm down after we get upset and teaches them that they don't have to react from fear-based emotions that the amygdala produces.

I believe MindUp is a program that can literally change the world. Goldie Hawn and her team are tirelessly working to bring this program into every school in the world. I encourage you to check out The Hawn Foundation at www.thehawnfoundation.org to learn more.

Another organization called The Holistic Life Foundation (www.hlfinc.org), founded by Ali Smith, Atman Smith, and Andres Gonzalez, teaches children yoga, mindfulness, and other mentoring practices.

CHAPTER 4

USE YOUR MIND TO CHANGE YOUR LIFE

So much of what happens in life depends on how you feel at any given moment. This is true whether you are a professional athlete, CEO of a company, or a bank teller. We are all influenced by emotional feelings and unconscious behaviors from our immediate social group as well as the media. This is a mere fact of being human. But you don't need to be at the whim of all that swirls around you. You can change your life by changing you mind. Meditation helps you to recognize your mind's operations in a clear and focused manner, so you can begin to make important changes in your life.

OUR PERCEPTION MODELS

Every thought that we have is merely a crap shoot at the casino. In other words, our thoughts are random and, at best, the result of our highly biased perceptions of what is out there. Our perceptual models of reality are not reliable.

In other words: *Your thoughts are not reality.* And, to take that one step further, let me say this: *YOU are not your thoughts!*

That we continually buy into our random thoughts and perceptions—our "mental model"—as if it is the one true reality—is what hinders us in life. People have the thought, *I'm too fat,* and then get caught up in an endless loop that has them possibly becoming anorexic. Differences in perception are the cause of almost every conflict on the planet. One person looks at the world through his or her own set of reality lenses and is unable to see through the reality lenses of another.

We each have our own unique worldview. We know that a person's mental model is something that is malleable due to countless stories of people radically changing into different people overnight. Think of North Korean prisons during the Korean War when the North Koreans brainwashed American prisoners of war. They used various techniques to slowly get U.S. prisoners to believe in the ideologies of North Korea. It worked so well, that, to this day, there are still American POWs who believe they are North Koreans.

The fact is that you can become conscious of your mind and then be aware of how it takes you to both places of genius and places of danger at the same. Meditation is the tool that can help you watch your thinking and therefore put you in a position to choose to change your life.

MIND OVER MATTER

How you think—negatively or positively—has a huge impact on every aspect of your life. When you are focused in your mind on the worst things that could happen in your day, your brain and body get fixed in a *fight-or-flight* response. This keeps you in a chronic state of stress by sending a cascade of stress hormones throughout your body. According to a study at the University of Pittsburgh as reported in the magazine *Men's Health,* negative thinkers have higher blood pressure and triglycerides than people who think positively. Negative thinkers also have higher odds of having a heart attack and premature death.

Thinking positively has a very different range of effects. A recent international study done at the Institute for the Psychology of Elite Performance in Wales showed that cyclists who used positive self-talk during a ride were able to extend their recovery rate by 18 percent. They used these key phrases in the study like *Feeling good* or *You're doing good.* When they started to get fatigued, they used words like *Keep going.*

Furthermore, according to a Mayo Clinic report, positive self-talk has been shown to increase life span, reduce risk of cardiovascular disease, lower rates of depression, lower levels of distress, and fight off a cold.

THE MIND IS CONSTANTLY CHANGING

Your mind is not a fixed thing; it is constantly changing. Even throughout a single day, your mind flips around, changing from happy to sad, from focused to unfocused. Eastern philosophy has brought light to the nature of the human mind for thousands of years. Through the efforts of masters, the practice of meditation became associated with a spiritual tradition, but it is also one of the greatest tools ever devised by man for self-improvement. In all areas of life, meditation has proven to be invaluable; the Taoists and Samurais used it to cook and do art, as well as to perfect their martial arts. We can use it to control our thinking and change our lives.

In the past three decades, thanks to new technology, the scientific field of neuroscience has revealed a tremendous amount of information about how the brain operates. A lot of this knowledge came from studies of traumatic brain injury in people who have damaged a part of their brain and lost certain abilities.

Neuroscientist and author Antonio D'amasio writes about a patient named Elliot who had a tumor removed from one of his frontal lobes in his book, *Descartes' Error: Emotion, Reason, and the Human Brain.* Prior to having the tumor removed, Elliot was a great husband and did incredibly well financially. After the tumor was removed, Elliott had trouble making decisions. His IQ was tested and shown to be phenomenal; however, he could not make a single decision about the simplest thing. At the grocery store, he could read every label but never picked out a box of cereal. He could never choose the right restaurant, because he'd have to drive to each one to read the menu. Eventually, a con man ripped him off, and he ended up losing his business. Worst of all, he got a divorce and had to move in with his parents—all because his ability to make decisions was nil.

UNCONSCIOUS TO OURSELVES

In his book *Strangers to Ourselves: Discovering the Adaptive Unconscious,* Timothy D. Wilson points out that our unconscious mind takes in over 11 million pieces of information, yet we are only conscious of 40 pieces of information per second.

Most of us are totally unconscious of the brain processes that run our lives.

In a sense, because of your changing mind, you are literally several different people, even though you think you are just one individual person. Most people act differently at church than they act at a party. We all see the world from a different point of view. The most important point of all the scientific studies done on the mind is for you to become aware of this process. The fact that we can become conscious of this process and therefore change it speaks volumes about our potential to completely change directions in our lives.

A study published in the *Journal of Personality and Social Psychology,* done at University of Rochester suggested that people who practice mindfulness have a better understanding of their emotions, and are more attune with their interests and values. By using mindfulness as a tool, you can recognize the blind spots that are causing problems in your life. For example, maybe you aren't treating everyone you meet with the respect they deserve. Maybe you are getting into frequent arguments with your spouse. You could use mindfulness to help you shift your focus onto the positive aspects of your life.

Every thought, every single emotion that you experience in your daily life can become just as addictive as any drug out there. The key is to constantly monitor these reactions and be able to differentiate them from who you are.

Your thoughts—and feelings—are not who you are!

Memory: Seeing into the Matrix of the Brain

One of the greatest benefits of meditation is to improve your memory. I don't mean just having greater recall of important facts, but also having the ability to not let memories of the past color your life in a negative way.

Your memory is not a videotape recorder; in essence, your memory is not 100% accurate. When you retrieve a memory, that memory is highly suggestible and malleable. A lot of torment comes from memories we hold of the past, and I want you to be able to see the truth of the process as it unfolds.

Let's take a look at that process of memory. There are two basic kinds of memory. The first is *implicit,* the ability that allows you to learn how to shoot a three-pointer in a basketball game unconsciously. The second, *explicit* memory, is the ability to look back and see how you played in a specific basketball game.

Explicit memory has to do with facts and events, such as the Chicago Bulls won the NBA championship in 1992, I went to Australia in 2009, etc. Implicit memory is memory that is used for unconscious processes, such as learning how to throw a baseball or drive a car. Both of these memory systems exchange information back and forth. For example, later in the book, you will learn some meditation forms, and, at first, you will have to read and go through all the mechanics. Later, those forms will become unconscious, and you won't have to think about them to do them. This is an example of how these memory systems work together.

Athletes, through their experiences and their brains' capacity of neuroplasticity, create neural networks that form what we call "memory." (Of course, this is an over-simplification for such a complex process!) How you remember something—that is, memory retrieval—occurs when you have a feeling or thought, or by an external cue from your environment.

When you recall a memory, your mind doesn't always know it's coming from the past. A lot of problems in life come from faulty implicit memories of the past. For example, if you were bitten by a dog, your brain might assume that all dogs are bad, which definitely isn't the case. But we also have good implicit memories; for example, your father might have treated people very well, so you might treat them well. The point is implicit memories run unconsciously in the background of our brain.

Unfortunately, this is the same process that causes all sorts of problems for people who are suffering from something called Post Traumatic Stress Disorder (PTSD). Their brain is constantly bombarded with implicit memories that don't always serve them well. In a restaurant, when a waiter drops a cup, such sufferers of PTSD may assume that the loud sound is a gunshot that happened on a previous tour of duty in Iraq. One method being used to help veterans is taking them through a virtual reality scenario to help them change their implicit memories. Another method being used is mindfulness meditation.

By recognizing the faulty behaviors in our life, we can come to realize that they are most likely formed from bad implicit memories that we installed throughout our lives. Your memories are not you, which is why several eastern traditions say meditation helps you to recognize your "true self." By achieving your "meditation muscle," you can recognize these patterns and go beyond them. The more meditation you do, the more you will be able to recognize faulty memories and other feelings. You can use your "meditation muscle" to examine those implicit memories and make them explicit memories. By making them explicit, you bring them to conscious awareness and realize that they are causing unnecessary behaviors in your life.

BRAIN MODELS OF REALITY

When we look at the world, we use both our logical and emotional brains. The emotional brain tends to automatically appraise possibilities in our environment. Without this ability, our species wouldn't have survived. The emotional brain makes rapid judgments, a capacity humans have used for thousands of years in a kind of trial and error fashion, hence shaping our perceptions.

The human brain forms models of reality and then perceives the world through these models of reality. This is a cause of much racism, depression, and unnecessary conflict in the world. We buy into these models of reality and then, if someone doesn't believe our model of reality, we don't like them, and will even fight them. Mindful meditation helps by having you begin to reconsider how your brain constructs reality, so you can witness its operations and then be effective at changing it.

As human beings, we operate from our beliefs about something and then, from those beliefs, build our model of the world around us based on them. The frightening part of that inherent human behavior is that we are not even conscious that we do this. It happens on a totally unconscious level, deceiving us into thinking that our beliefs are the reality.

Once again, modern brain science to the rescue!

Neuroscience has begun to shed light on how memories are stored. Your brain stores only the essence of an experience. It is not a video camera that stores exact detail of an event. Recent research has pointed out that our memories are extremely malleable in that you tend to remember an event based about how you feel in the present moment. Every time you access a memory, it based upon how you currently feel at the time you are accessing it. That is why they say an eyewitness account is extremely temperamental, not always to be counted upon.

So just where is consciousness located in the brain? No one really knows with a hundred percent certainty. But neuroscientists do know that a piece of the puzzle lies in the synaptic connections within the brain. If you close your eyes and visualize an ocean, an integrated network of connected neurons fires off in order to produce the emotions and sight of the ocean you see. The more you visualize an ocean—or physically see an ocean, for that matter—the stronger those connections get.

Neurons that fire together, wire together.

We are constantly updating our neural networks; depending on what we do, we update our neural networks all the time. At University of Wisconsin-Madison Richard Davidson and colleagues studied meditators who had over 10,000 hours of practice and they were able to produce massive gamma waves that are associated with well-being. These long term meditators most likely have larger areas of neural networks dedicated to meditation, compared to the brain of an average person who never meditated before.

The point I am making is that we do not experience the environment itself but rather a projection of it. The University of Bordeaux did a study on how the brain sees, and the eyes do not. Researchers dropped odorless, tasteless, red dye into glasses of white wine and then gave the wine to 54 wine-tasting experts. Not one of them could tell the wine had been altered—they all believed they were drinking red wine.

One of the key aspects of several traditions of meditation is to become more conscious of automatic processes that go on in the mind. Only then we can begin to be aware of such processes and change them. A lot of problems in life stem from the fact that we become stuck in a particular pattern. The goal is to notice our faulty patterns and work with the mind to shift them.

The following activity will help you to begin to become objective about your thoughts and feelings so you can alter faulty patterns that result from them.

ACTIVITY: TAKING MENTAL SELFIES WITHOUT YOUR SMARTPHONE

Pause throughout the day and take a mental selfie of your thoughts. Spend one minute a day for one week jotting down the random thoughts and feeling you have in a journal. You'll find that most of your thoughts are random, including much old stuff you've had running around your head through the years.

When you are able to separate from your thoughts, you will see massive changes in your life. Many of your problems stem from letting your thoughts and feelings get the best of you— *as if they were you.* You can recover from the most devastating career and personal setbacks when you are able to become the witness of your thoughts and feelings, not the victim of them.

ARE YOU GOING TO RUN YOUR MIND OR IS YOUR MIND GOING TO RUN YOU?

How many times a day are you tormented by things that happened in the past by people you trusted and sometimes even loved? We tend to hang on to things that no longer serve us, a major pattern that weighs everyone down.

The key to really letting go is to truly forgive. We have to face all sorts of emotions as we go through life; some of them are lovely, and some of them are downright terrible. In your meditations, you may encounter people who've harmed you—this is normal. But it is also a time to learn to forgive them and accept that they did what they did. When you don't forgive and hold on to grief and resentment, the only person you are hurting is yourself.

LETTING GO MEDITATION

1. Begin with breathing from your diaphragm.
2. Cultivate the emotions of forgiveness and loving kindness.
3. Visualize and reframe the photos and emotions in your mind from negative to positive
4. It doesn't matter what the person did to you. Visualize yourself forgiving the person while cultivating the emotion of forgiveness.
5. Open your eyes and carry this feeling with you through your day.

MIND AND BODY

Many Eastern traditions of medicine are keenly aware of how the mind affects the body. One of the core aspects of Traditional Chinese medicine is to monitor your thinking, because it is the belief that thoughts translate into disease. The same belief system holds true in Ayurveda which is the ancient health system of India. Western science now knows that stress causes massive problems to our wellbeing.

From the recent advancements in neuroscience, we know that the brain produces chemicals that influence the body. Scientists also know the body produces chemicals that influence the brain. Every idea that we have about life, every thought and emotion we feel, produces a chemical reaction in the mind and body. The English word *emotion* is derived from the French word *émouvoir,* meaning "to stir up." This is the kind of fire inside that caused Michelangelo to paint the Sistine Chapel or caused Beethoven to spend thousands of hours on concertos working out the perfect melody. Emotions are fuel for wonderful things to happen, but they have also been the fire that burnt people's lives to the ground. This nearly happened to Abraham Lincoln's life, due to his life-long battle with depression. Although some would argue that Abe was a manic depressive, because of his amazing resilience, he turned into a powerful force to change the world.

WARRIOR MONKS

Monks in Eastern monasteries used sophisticated meditation techniques to train a warrior for battle. They had an entire curriculum set up for this purpose, emphasizing the need to be separate from thoughts and emotions. A young warrior trainee was first introduced to meditation by learning how to monitor his breathing by putting his tongue at the palate of his mouth and breathing from his nose to his abdomen. Then he was given a calligraphy brush and told to make circles with it, all the while staying in a completely meditative state. From there, he slowly evolved into doing other forms of meditative activity, such as gardening, farming, and cooking. Everything was done in a meditative frame of mind. The head monk would monitor the young student's progress and decide what work he would perform in the village. Some would be doctors, farmers, chiefs, warriors—all roles carried out in a calm, meditative state.

The purpose of practicing meditation in these cultures was to cultivate an ability to disengage the mind from its endless judgments, diversions, and other mental habits, and be present simply to what is *really* happening in the environment— not projections of what is happening. Once you are present, you can easily master anything. The "study" is in becoming aware of your immediate surroundings and responding to them purely.

The mind tends to continually wheel into different emotional states throughout the day, from happy to sad, from sad to excited. The mind is constantly changing from one emotional state to another, so you must not identify with our thoughts. *They are not who you are.*

4 WAYS TO PUT MEDITATION INTO YOUR LIFE RIGHT NOW

1. *Any place or time.* Close your eyes and bring your focus to your breathing. Let your thoughts go as they do, but return and continue to focus on your breathing in a controlled manner.
2. *At Work.* You can find ways to incorporate meditation into your work schedule, whether before, during, or after work. Try to bring your attention to your breathing whenever you feel stressed; this can be done at any time throughout the day. Another option for work time meditation is to take a few moments on your lunch break to sit quietly and watch your breath.
3. *Before You Exercise.* I find meditation to be immensely beneficial when used before exercising. If you're a runner, try to do at least 10 to 15 minutes of meditation right before you run. Then you can make your run a moving meditation.
4. *When You Wake Up.* If you do meditation close to the time you wake up in the morning, it will impact every area of your life during the day. Try to do a few minutes of meditation every morning before you start your day.

BECOME THE PILOT

Always remember that you are the pilot of your own mind. You are the one who watches the mind, and you have the ability to separate from your thoughts and feelings coming at you from your mind. Become best friends with this pilot who is your true awareness and self. Use this pilot to observe the workings of your mind without any perceived attachments to what your mind is doing. This is a daily practice that can be done to manage your emotional state throughout the day. Remember: *If you don't rule your brain, it will rule you!*

The key here is becoming separate from your mind and brain. The first goal is to recognize the pilot (or true self), and then to recognize the secondary emotions you are experiencing. For example, imagine you are driving along and the car in front of you stops suddenly to let a passenger out of the car. Instead of having a full-blown stress attack, recognize that the reaction you are having is something your brain and nervous system is doing. It is not who you are.

When you label your thoughts, feelings, and behaviors, you can then get enough space from them to change them. If you're anxious, just say the word: *anxious.* If you are excited, label your experience *excited.* You want to observe all the emotions going on in your body. This is something you can do all day if you want to steer how you feel on any given day. By doing this, you get better at knowing and changing yourself.

CHAPTER 5

WORKOUT FOR THE MIND: PURE YI MEDITATION

If you grow up and go to school in America, one of the first things you're taught in physical education class is how to do a push-up. Millions of Americans do push-ups before work, during their lunch break, and at the gym. Because of push-ups, many have been able to master getting ripped pectorals, deltoids, and triceps. At the least, many of us have gotten tighter abs.

The push-up is an incredible tool to help you get in great physical shape, which is why it's used in almost every gym in America. However, what about getting in great mental shape? With all the scientific evidence pointing to the many mental and emotional benefits of meditation, the practice is literally becoming America's first popular mental exercise—push-ups for the brain. Just as the push-up has been a standard part of being American, meditation is becoming a standard as America's newest workout for the brain.

MENTAL FLAB: STRESS

While the gyms are full of people doing push-ups, our national state–affected by stress and its consequences–is not faring so well. This is especially apparent in the business world where stress costs American businesses around $300 billion a year.

Several of my friends who are driven, business-savvy men and women with Type A personalities like to tease me about practicing meditation. This continued until one Friday night, when a friend pulled me aside and said, "Hey, I have really bad stress problems. Can you tell me about meditation?" In fact, he wasn't the first of my friends to do this; I've heard the same line from a few of them.

Another friend lives in an expensive high rise in Chicago and works 100 hours week. When I stopped by to visit him, he opened the door, looking like he hadn't slept in a week. My first words were, "Stressed out?" He responded, "Yeah, incredibly stressed."

Stressed lifestyles seem to be a part of American culture: everything is go, go, go! No wonder the majority of heart attacks in America occur on Monday morning, the beginning of the workweek. Another guy I know had Band-Aids on his thumbs from typing so many emails on his BlackBerry. He types more than 100 emails a day and the skin on his thumbs was actually peeling off. He was so stressed that it was difficult just to have a conversation with him.

It seems like this fable of the lion and gazelle is permanently installed into the psyche of American culture: *Every morning in Africa, a gazelle wakes up and knows it must outrun the fastest lion or it will be killed. Every morning in Africa, a lion wakes up. The lion knows it must run faster than the slowest gazelle, or it will starve. It doesn't matter whether you're the lion or a gazelle; when the sun comes up, you'd better be running.*

You don't have to live like this!

I teach meditation to a number of Type A personalities, and one of the things I see is that many of them have forgotten how to breathe. The first thing I teach them is to breathe naturally. It's possible to be successful and relaxed at the same time if we, as a culture, incorporate meditation into everyday life. There's nothing wrong with a culture full of ambitious men and women; I just want to see more people relaxed and enjoying life.

The millions of Americans who exercise could be meditating before and after they jump on the treadmill. Why is this not the norm? There's no question we all need exercise, not just for physical health, but also for the positive changes in your brain. A tremendous amount of research explains how physical exercise strengthens the brain and even works as good as an anti-depressant to alleviate relevant symptoms. We are biologically designed to do physical exercise; hence, we get a great feeling after we do it. What some call a "runner's high" is caused by a chemical in the brain, *endorphins*, that makes you want to do it again. Exercise has been associated with better sex, higher productivity, increased immune function, and longevity.

Nonetheless, many still choose to sit on the couch, rather than go to the gym and exercise. We are meant to move, not to sit in a chair all day. One study is saying that sitting is an epidemic comparable to smoking. Too much sitting contributes to severe back pain as well as cardiovascular problems.

Standing Moving Meditation. When I find myself sitting a lot, I will get up and do a few minutes of walking meditation to balance out all the sitting. I recommend you do this whenever you get a chance. Moving meditation helps you to flow, and, when you flow, everything just works better. There's a reason why if you go into any major park in China, millions of people are doing moving meditation practices such as Tai Chi or Qigong. The government encourages the practice because of all the positive health benefits they've recognized from the practice of standing moving meditation.

One of the greatest ways to enhance your exercise program is to use mindfulness meditation. Start a 3- to 5-minute meditation right before you go to the gym, and then, when you get home, do a little bit of meditation afterwards to help solidify those wonderful emotions in your body. I can't tell you how much better I feel when I do some meditation right after a workout.

So many people have adopted an iPod into their workout, bringing music into the world of exercise and making their workouts that more enjoyable. Meditation is just one more way to make working out fun. Even at work, people could be meditating before work as well as during their lunch break to stay focused. Ten years from now, the practice of meditation is going to be as commonplace as doing a push-up.

VISUALIZATION FOR A WORKOUT

I'm sure you've visualized how you could look and feel if you committed to a new workout regime—and you know that visualization can become real through the power of your brain. This is because the brain does not know the difference between what you visualize internally and what you see externally. To your brain, these are the same, as shown on fMRI scans when similar areas in the brain light up for both processes.

Here are some steps to practice:

1. Close your eyes and focus on your breathing.
2. Now visualize yourself running down a beach and allow yourself to feel everything you would feel if you were totally confident in your new body image. Feel how healthy you feel. Circulate these feelings throughout your entire body, feeling confident and satisfied.
3. Open your eyes and notice any change in your commitment to work out.

Meditation Made Easy

At the time of this writing, I've done over 15,000 hour of meditation, but you don't have to spend that amount of time to get the same benefits I've experienced. For people who can't do so many hours of meditation due to lifestyle or family and work commitments, I have adapted a system that works for someone who can devote only ten to twenty minutes a day to their practice.

I've searched all over the world for the best meditation systems and can personally attest to there being a multitude. In America alone, we have Transcendental Meditation, Mindfulness, Insight Meditation, Zen, Vipassana, Tibetan Buddhist meditation, Taoist meditation, as well as practices that incorporate meditation, such as yoga, *pranayama*, Tai Chi, and Qigong.

The two meditation practices I focus on manifest in two different meditative modes: sitting (practiced as mindfulness) and moving (practiced as Tai Chi and Qigong). I have synthesized a curriculum based on both modes from a traditional Taoist temple meditation system. I did not invent this system. The entire curriculum is based on my nine-and-half years of private lessons with a Taoist monk and several other teachers. In my adapted system, I've removed any type of religious attachment to the art.

Let's take a look at the two main kinds of meditation I teach, *mindfulness meditation* and *moving meditation*.

Mindfulness Meditation

According to Jon Kabat-Zinn, one of the leading pioneers of mindfulness meditation, as quoted in his book *Wherever You Go, There You Are*, "Mindfulness means paying attention in a particular way; on purpose, in the present moment, and non-judgmentally." Mindfulness has no religious elements attached to it and has been used in mainstream American healthcare, the U. S. military, and in public education.

Mindfulness is a state of awareness cultivated by focusing your attention on the present moment. It means to have the ability to train your focus towards the present. Most of our activities rob us of our focus; even some forms of habitual thinking steal our focus. You can notice this when you are sitting with someone at dinner, and your mind starts to travel while the person talking. Mindfulness is the ability to bring your focus back to the person you're talking with.

Moreover, mindfulness is one of the most precious qualities of mind to have throughout your day, informing all of your communications and other activities. Think how it would change your life if you could always "be here now." This means to not be thinking about your to-do list, but rather focusing your mind on being in the present moment. So many problems arise simply because we are not usually focused on the present moment.

ONE MINUTE MINDFULNESS MEDITATION

1. Sit in a chair with your spine straight. Loosen your belt if it's tight and close your eyes.
2. Focus on bringing your awareness to your breath. Observe all the various feelings in your body. Observe how you are breathing. Are you breathing fast or slow? Is your breathing getting caught or is it smooth and flowing?
3. If your mind is wandering, just bring your attention back to observing your breathing.
4. Open your eyes after one minute. Notice how you feel.

If you use mindfulness to still your mind and look at the various emotions that you deal with throughout the day, you'll have a much better quality of life. For example, anger, one of the most troubling and powerful emotions, can easily lead you in directions you don't want to go, like yelling at your friends, co-workers, or spouse. Mindful awareness helps you to recognize this emotion and not let it control your life. Hence, if you feel anger arising in your body, learn to focus your attention on your deep breathing from the belly. You'll notice that any anger dissipates quite readily when you do this.

MOVING MEDITATION: THE REAL THING

One of the biggest problems people encounter when starting a meditation practice is dealing with how to settle the mind. This same problem occurred over 2,500 years ago when Taoist monks were sitting still and trying to control their minds. All types of Eastern meditation systems have encountered this problem; some use *mantras* (a word, phrase, or symbol that is repeated) to help settle the mind. But through constant observation, Taoist monks realized that, in addition to sitting, they must also move in order to fully condition and still their minds. In my opinion, by far the greatest way to settle the mind and condition it in a positive way is through the practice of *moving meditation.*

This is the major difference between Taoist meditation and the more popular Buddhist meditation in the West— the emphasis on moving vs. sitting. However, as a result of the massive hit Taoist meditation took after the Cultural Revolution in China, when its practice was banned in that country, many systems like Tai Chi and Qigong became scattered, such that here in the West we only get a partial picture. The Taoist system I learned was taught to me in complete secrecy. It may sound strange, but, even recently, my lessons were taught only at my teacher's house, not at his school. I was taught a totally different curriculum than what was taught publicly.

A Taoist system contains sitting meditation, standing meditation, moving meditation, and reclining meditation, and it is based in an understanding of *energy*. I have 100 percent confidence that the next major breakthrough Western science will make is the discovery of an "energetic" system in the human body, made up of what Eastern traditions call the "life force." Similar to the nervous system and the human genome, an energetic system in the body will be discovered once we are able to measure it.

I know some people are turned off by airy-fairy talk about energy—*qi* in Eastern terms. However, it's just a matter of time before a Western scientist examines this phenomenon of the mind and validates it. The reason I touch on this subject is because I think you can reach incredible states of health, happiness, and life satisfaction by balancing your mind and learning to feel your own energy system at work.

SOME MYTHS ABOUT ENERGY

Energy is not just electricity, something which Western scientists have been able to measure for some time. The kind of energy you learn to feel during meditation is an internal, biodynamic phenomenon, a sense of life force coursing throughout your mind and body and potentially available for you to use and direct as you wish.

Energy is not just a matter of following your breath. Think of it this way: Your mind is energy that works in concert with your brain. And you don't have to have any spiritual beliefs in the validity of this energy system for it to be experienced. Most people who meditate long or hard enough eventually condition their mind and body to properly feel energy.

One simple way to feel energy is to establish your focus on the area just below your navel. Visualize this area being full of life force, expanding and throbbing with energy. In Taoist culture, many types of different verbal teachings existed to explain the phenomena of contacting energy in this way, including seeing yourself as nine months pregnant or visualizing that you have a moon in your belly and holding that image as the energy becomes more and more palpable.

ENERGY, INTUITION, AND INSTINCTS

Intuition and instincts are something we all have, recognizable as the "hunch" you get when you're in a dangerous situation. This very real and valuable feeling has kept humans alive for eons. Intuition and survival instincts are part of the machinery of our brains. Paul D. Maclean, a neuroscientist, coined the term "triune brain" to explain how the brain evolved over the years in three parts. The first area of the brain that holds intuition and our instincts is the "old brain" or "reptilian complex." The old brain is made up of the brain stem and cerebellum. The cerebellum is responsible for the "fight or flight" instincts, digestion, reproduction, circulation, and breathing. Moreover, the old brain influences survival behaviors, like social hierarchy, reproduction, and establishing territory. Most behaviors coming from this area of the brain are unconscious. How old is this part? Incredibly, you share this brain with reptiles like salamanders.

The next area of the brain, the limbic system, is also responsible for intuition and instinct; this area of the brain is responsible for feelings, memories and emotions. Dogs have limbic systems, and so do you. When I'm over at my parents' house, their dog, a Labrador Retriever (she might be mixed with something else) named "Izzy," will be upstairs sleeping, but, when she hears the garage door open, she will run down to greet them with a wagging tail. She also sits on the back porch scanning her territory; if a squirrel comes in her territory, she will chase it down. These are all responses coming from Izzy's "old brain" and limbic system.

The third area of the brain, the neo-cortex, has given me the ability to write this book; it's responsible for human language, abstract thought, imagination, and other learning capabilities. These three areas—the "old brain," the limbic system, and the neo-cortex—have strong neural connections, so as to work in unison. Neuroscientists now also know that we have neural networks surrounding areas of the intestines and heart, lending new credence to the term "gut feeling." These neural networks communicate with the brain and may be what gives us our intuition.

I state all of this information to suggest that we are intuitive animals; these gut feelings we have are real. We can navigate this world by focusing on our feelings, and we can make better decisions if we listen to the feelings in our body and become more mindful.

For example, when Taoist monks and Samurai warriors needed to protect a village, they would place someone outside to guard and scan the mountain range. The guards would often operate in a meditative state, and whenever they got a "gut feeling," they would act on it. Students training as monks had done various meditative practices in order to hone in on this gut feeling. To start, everything in their daily life was done from such a gut feeling. As soon as they woke up in the morning, they were taught to focus on their *dan tein* or *hara*. Through meditation, they extended their gut feeling into cooking, sword-making, farming, etc.

In some Taoist practices, students use a wooden staff that is several feet long and train their mind to focus at the end of the staff, with the goal of extending their energy and mind to that point. It's my opinion this works because your mind is an energy field and what you focus on influences everything around you. While such a view breaks from all current Western scientific models, it is an idea borrowed from Eastern cultures. At some point, I think this *energy field* can and will be measured by Western science, probably with quantum mechanics or some other scientific model not yet discovered. I look forward to the day when someone wins a Nobel Prize for formulating a scientific model around this energy field that Eastern traditions have been based on since ancient times.

Even though we have no scientific proof yet, intuition and extended energy fields of the human mind are very real. Every culture from the Native Americans to the Greeks had various ways to use intuition. For example, the Moken people of Thailand lived through the 2004 tsunami. It was one of the greatest tsunami disasters in history; over 200,000 people died in this disaster. However, most of the Moken people survived because they were able to witness and feel changes in the ocean. By using intuition, they knew that a tsunami was coming and they would need to get to higher ground.

They saw that the ocean was "misbehaving," so they went up to higher ground and thus survived. Many animals also didn't die because they were able to use their intuition to foresee the coming event.

Your intuition is real. It has been around for millions of years, helping animals. I often hear people say things like, *The energy just isn't right.* Or that some event or person has *great energy.* Your emotional system is extraordinarily complex, and that energy you feel intuitively can and should be honed.

INTUITION AND MEDITATION

The meditation program I teach you helps you to strengthen your awareness and intuitive feeling. Taoist monks who practiced what I teach lived in the wild, sometimes on top of mountains, meditating all day to strengthen their intuition as a survival mechanism. For example, if a monk were walking in the wilderness, he would want to know if a tiger was near. While walking, he would be meditating, extending his awareness out into the wilderness, being mindfully aware of the feelings going on in his body.

In the meditation practice of Tai Chi, you learn to keep your focus on "infinity," trying to utilize your maximum output of awareness. You train to expand your body's sensitivity out into the world, so you can pick up more cues in your environment. Taoist monks would meditate out in nature and connect energetically with the environment, the trees, the sun, and the breeze, enhancing their ability to survive.

Much unconscious knowledge comes from the "gut." As you'll see in Pure Yi, I'm constantly emphasizing bringing your attention to the area of your gut. Western science is now starting to recognize some fascinating insights coming from the enteric nervous system in the gut. According to an article in the *Harvard Mental Health Letter*, the enteric nervous system is sometimes referred to as "the second brain." The enteric nervous system uses neurotransmitters to send signals to the central nervous system. One of these neurotransmitters is serotonin, a chemical often associated with happiness.

This type of unconscious knowledge also comes from experience. Firefighters who have been fighting fires for years have a deep intuition about how fires work. They have trained the sensory regions of their brain. In effect, they have become more sensitive to their environment on an intuitive level, and they develop an unconscious knowledge about how the fire is moving and where to go.

This phenomena may be explained by what scientists are calling *von economo neurons,* brain cells now known to occur in parts of the brain that process sensations and social emotions. Some neuroscientists believe that these are part of our "intuition neurons." We sometimes forget that we have the same brains as animals, the main difference between us and apes being that we have larger frontal lobes. We go back and forth analyzing intuition and rationality. The goal is to focus on bringing our "meditation muscle" in line with our feelings as much as possible throughout the day.

PURE YI

In the system I have designed and call Pure Yi, the foundation for practice is moving meditation. This system is based on my nine-and-a-half years of private lessons with a Taoist monk and with several other masters. I removed all the religious aspects of the system. It's a system over 2,500 years old, yet it is simple and accessible for anyone today.

I've seen many systems that claim to use forms of moving meditation, but the movements taught are incredibly fast and difficult to master. In my system, you go incredibly slow—the slower the better. Sometimes you close your eyes and sometimes you keep them open, depending on how you feel. You focus on your breathing, and stay in a state of continual, *slow* motion. A part of my system was designed by warrior monks who meditated most of the day as a way to prepare for battle and needed a system not only for battle but for self-preservation.

Pure Yi fuses three great traditions: Mindfulness, Tai Chi, and Qigong. Moreover, it consists of five types of meditation: moving, sitting, reclining, standing, and mindful awareness.

Throughout your training in my system, you are constantly applying the following principles:

1. *Focused awareness.* You train your mind to have greater control over your attention (mindfulness).
2. *Inner focus.* By focusing within, you learn to recognize positive emotions, feeling your heart beat, your breathing, and every organ in your body.
3. *Flowing movement.* You are always moving and flowing from posture to posture, sometimes very subtly.

4. *Mental intention.* Your mental intent drives the movements of your body, and the goal is to achieve a pure, clear mind. Visualization is a major part of intent.
5. *Breath control.* You practice full, deep diaphragmatic breathing, more specifically, breathing from your *dan tein*, an energy center located just below your navel.
6. *Relaxation.* You are relaxing your muscles when doing any exercise, relieving as much tension as possible.

In my studies, I also came to realize that there are so many forms and complicated structures in Tai Chi that it is difficult for Western people to remember them all. I've studied several of the family styles of Tai Chi, including *Yang, Chen,* and *Wu,* but, when I began teaching, I saw my students were getting frustrated trying to remember the many forms. The goal of Tai Chi is not to do the correct form, but to train the mind, and having to remember so many forms was short-circuiting that goal.

It's common for people to be introduced to meditation, try it a few times, and then quit because it's too difficult. For this reason, I emphasize moving meditation in Pure Yi, because it makes the practice more accessible. Instead of remembering many different forms, students simply close their eyes and attend to their breath, intention, and body movement.

The six principles applied in Pure Yi are given here in detail:

PRINCIPLE # 1: FOCUSED AWARENESS

A house must have a strong foundation in order to last, and the same is true of your practice in this method. A foundational process I borrow from Eastern philosophy is the theory of *ying* and *yang,* which says that everything must come into the proper balance. American culture is a society that is aggressive and career-driven, needing the yin side of life to balance it. Yin is focused on kindness, compassion, and well-being. In Pure Yi, you are always balancing ying and yang interactions in your body. For example, yang would be the movement, and yin would be the stillness.

The goal here is to have a clear and focused mind. You may have had the experience of being on a hike in the wilderness and, after a while, looked up to notice everything is totally clear in the sky. Moving meditation will help you to achieve this kind of clear and serene mind. I base my method on Traditional Chinese medicine, which says that, although you may hear mental chatter in your brain, your actual mind is both inside your head and outside it in a greater field of awareness.

Shifting Feet exercise: A simple way to regain your focus and clear your mind is to close your eyes and shift your weight back and forth from foot to foot. In doing this, you establish a clear understanding of the ying and yang. For example, if you shift your weight to your right leg, your right leg is yang, your left leg is yin. If you then shift your weight to your left leg, your left leg is yang, your right leg is yin.

PRINCIPLE # 2: INNER FOCUS

How would you hold a 6-month-old baby? The answer: *very gently*! When you look within, treat yourself as gently as you would a tiny baby. Become aware of everything inside: your heartbeat, your liver, the various tensions in your body. Also, feel the various emotions in your body, no matter what they are. In doing this, you are using mindfulness awareness.

Focusing on what's going on inside your body, both physically and emotionally, can also help you to recover from pains or ailments you may be dealing with. When you focus on the pain, you can work to flow through it and release it. In Traditional Chinese medicine, when meridians (pathways of energy in the body) are blocked, disease results. For thousands of years, Taoist warrior cultures have used moving meditation to open energy blockages to maintain health and well-being.

Western science is now beginning to shed light on exactly how our thoughts and emotions can impact our health and well-being. Our thoughts have real, tangible effects on our body, especially over the long term, a concept that was built into the Eastern systems thousands of years ago. Monks were always looking for ways to balance the inner working of their minds through meditation. Today's science tells us that practicing mindfulness helps to shift activation away from the right prefrontal cortex to the left side of the prefrontal cortex, the side that has been shown to be associated with more positive emotions.

I often experience how moving meditation changes my thinking when I walk out of a session with a totally different mindset than when I went in—one that is focused and ready to take on the day.

PRINCIPLE # 3: MOVEMENT

What separates Pure Yi from every other method of meditation is the movement. In my experience, moving is by far the best way to meditate. The mind is like a wild animal, and several types of meditation use different ways to tame it. Some use mantras, and some use simple breathing. In Pure Yi, we use: mindfulness, breath, and movement.

The monks who originally designed the system of movement meditation realized that the universe is always interacting with both yin and yang forces. For example, the sun is shining which is yin; but when the sun goes down, the moon rises, which is yang. In Traditional Chinese medicine, the doctor is always looking to balance the yin and yang energies in the body for optimal health.

An important movement principle in Pure Yi that incorporates this is called "opening and closing." For example, when you move out in a form you are *opening*, and when you move in you are *closing*. Notice how a baby breathes from the belly, inhaling to *open* (the belly rises) and exhaling to *close* (the belly drops.) That same principle is imbedded into my method. Every movement you make has an *open* and *close* component: the yin and the yang.

This "open and close" principle can help you establish a consistent flow of movement in your life. Several factors can influence this flow, including your diet, your thoughts, and even changes in the weather. You perform at your peak when you are in the flow, and everything is relaxed in a focused state. I teach people this moving meditation in the morning so they can flow easier through their work day. If you do a solid 20 to 40 minute practice in the morning, you can experience mindfulness throughout the day, making your life smoother and more relaxed. In Traditional Chinese medicine, it's believed that if the energy is flowing smoothly in your body, then you'll be healthy.

Flow starts with having your mindful awareness activated at a level where you won't be thrown off from the pushes and pulls that occur throughout the day. We now know that positive thinking has a major impact on the quality of your life. If you're stuck in negative thinking all day, you are sending signals to your body that may be upsetting this balance, so it's important to recognize and visualize positive emotions.

In my training with monks, I was taught a form called the "water form." Monks stood by the ocean and observed how a wave comes in and hits the shoreline. They then mimic this pattern of the waves in a flowing, moving meditation.

Psychologist and author Mihaly Csikszentmihalyi used the term "flow" to describe optimal states of performance. He studied cultures from all over the world and saw that the people who thrived in society are the one who found a state of flow. When artists are in their optimal state, they are in a flow mindset. Flow is the ability to be completely immersed in what you are doing. For example, if you are a writer in the flow, you are channeling your focus into whatever you're writing. Taoist monks stayed in the flow, achieving a zen-like state in all of their work, for example, the art and science of sword making.

A Taoist Tai Chi sword was fashioned only after the sword-maker meditated for hours, enabling him to go into a "flow" state to work on the sword. During the process, whenever the sword-maker dropped out of a flow state, he would stop and return back into meditation. A similar method was used for Samurai sword-making and in several Eastern arts, such as tea harvesting and sushi making, requiring the person to apprentice with an expert or master for up to ten years.

I've incorporated the same approach in some of my activities. For example, when I write, I practice getting into the flow. I'm constantly going off track, so, to refocus, I pause, close my eyes, do a few minutes of meditation, and then return to my writing. I also do this several times as I move through the day. In the nine-and-a-half years I've been studying moving meditation, I must have heard the word *flow* over a thousand times, reminding me to flow with it all, no matter what it is I encounter.

Instead of taking on life directly, try flowing with it. Picture your mind as water; water can get dirty and murky when it is stagnant. When it flows, it cleans itself. The same thing happens with your mind. If you find yourself in a stagnant place in life, make sure to refocus on getting back into the flow. Start with flowing in meditation, and then take that flow into your life's activities. Flow even with the obstacles as they may come up, because, no matter who you are or what circumstances you are dealing with, obstacles will appear in your life.

Principle # 4: Mental Intention

In Pure Yi, your *intention* drives the movements of your body. You flow from one form to another form, but your mental intent moves your body, as, when switching from one form to another, you visualize the movement before you move. Your mind is a field of pure energy, and you are moving that field to make a movement in your body.

In my method, you are essentially training your intention. Later on, you will be able use your focused intention to guide not only your body but more positive states of mind. The theory of focused intention is not new, nor did I invent it; rather, it is a several-thousand-year-old principle that I borrowed from Eastern martial arts, Eastern philosophies, and Traditional Chinese medicine.

Principle # 5: Breath control

Your breath is your life—you cannot live without it. True mindful awareness occurs first with befriending your breath. Your breath is your greatest friend in navigating the ups and downs in life. By focusing your wandering attention back on to your breath, it helps you be in the moment and present to your surroundings. Most of us aren't even conscious of our breath, as we're so focused on our daily to-do list, our cell phones, and the many other day-to-day distractions that come up.

Here is a simple mindfulness exercise to help your notice your breath: Stop what you are doing right now and take one full deep diaphragm breath in and one full deep diaphragm breath out. Now, keep your mind totally open and become aware of your surroundings. Take in all the feelings and sensations in your body and in your mind with this open awareness.

What was that like?

When you begin to notice your breath, you will understand how unconscious you become when doing activities throughout the day. Awareness is everything in your life, and the simple act of noticing awareness is the key to have more control over your life.

In a moving meditation, you fuse mindfulness and breath as one, so, on each movement, you inhale and exhale. Taoists observed animals and babies in order to come up with their methods. For example, they saw that frogs expand and contract their bodies when they breathe. This essentially is what you are doing by expanding on the inhale and contracting on the exhale when you breathe.

The unique thing about breathing is that it can be done both consciously and unconsciously. You can consciously become aware of your breathing and use it to influence your bodily functions. The in and out, open and close meditation principles I speak of help you specifically to do this.

PRINCIPLE # 6: RELAXATION

If you remember one word and one word only from this chapter, it should be *relax*. When you're doing moving meditation, you aren't strengthening your muscles; you are relaxing it. As you meditate and relax, you'll recognize all the different emotions that go along with the practice. Imagine you're getting a personal massage without a masseuse—that's how relaxed you can become. You may become so relaxed, you feel as if you have no bones in your body.

Our American culture values activities that strengthen bodies, not relax them. Whenever I coach someone, the first thing I have to tell them and repeat over and over again is to relax. Even when I tell people this, they still continue to tense their muscles in the process of starting a form. After years of conditioning from learning how to lift weights, learn routines like changing tires, lifting boxes, etc., we think every activity must be done with maximum strength. However, in this system, remember, you're meditating. Your aim is to *let go,* not become stronger. Build muscle after or before you do this practice, but not during it.

With every movement and every breath in Pure Yi, you will find yourself relaxing more and more. In Traditional Chinese Medical, such relaxation opens the energy channels in the body to facilitate healing. It is also thought to massage the internal organs, keeping them vital and clear. When you begin to do moving meditation, you will find that this relaxed feeling stays with you throughout your day.

EXERCISES TO PRACTICE MOVEMENT MEDITATION

It's now time for you to try some moving meditation forms and experience for yourself the six principles you just read about. Choose a quiet location in your home or out in nature, and wear loose clothing to begin your practice. Then move through the following exercises in the order they are given:

Exercise 1: *Vertical Circle Stance*. This meditative form coordinates and relaxes the upper and lower extremities of the body.

Begin by relaxing your shoulders, hips, knees, ankles, and feet. You will be meditating constantly while performing this exercise; you can have your eyes closed, or 30% to 50% open, or completely open. I recommend starting with your eyes about 30% open.

Place your feet shoulder-width apart and make sure your hips, chest, and shoulders are relaxed. Keep your focus on meditating and breathing from your abdomen, inhaling and exhaling two to three times. Lift the crown of your head and slightly bend and relax your knees. Then, slowly raise your hands, starting with your fingertips, followed by your wrist, and then your forearms. When your fingers reach nose-height, slowly begin to descend, starting with your elbows, followed by your forearms and wrist.

When descending, you are gently sinking with your whole body. When you do these movements, you want to move with your entire body while trying to keep your senses totally open to all the sensations in your body, such as heart beat, the feeling of your nose, ears, toes, elbows, etc. The more you can feel, the better.

Do this exercise 5 to 15 times, matching your inhale to when you are rising and your exhale when you are descending.

Principles to remember:

- Focus on meditation and relaxation first; the form is secondary.
- Don't tense any area of your body.
- Focus on deep, full diaphragmatic breathing.

Exercise 2: *Expand-Contract.* This form works on opening and relaxing the hip and shoulder joints while relaxing your mind.

Begin diaphragmatic breathing, placing your hands a few inches away from your stomach to remind you to breathe from that area. From this position, extend your elbows out to start the movement, which is followed by your forearm, wrist, and then fingers. The right hand and your left hand fingers match each other, as if you're carrying a bowl of water. At all times, keep the knees relaxed. On the up movement, you're lifting lightly with the crown of your head (imagine a string pulling the top of your head up very lightly).

When you get to shoulder-height, open and rotate your arms outward. Your palms will now be facing the ground a little bit below shoulder width, and, as you descend, sink down while relaxing. You may notice yourself tensing up, and, if so, bring your awareness back to relaxing. Also, if your mind wanders, bring your attention back to the mindful movement that you're doing.

Exercise 3: *Legs Shifting Back and Forth.*

This is an important form for relaxing and opening your hips, knees, ankles, and feet. You can do this at any time throughout your day. It's a great to do in the office when you want to focus and do a short moving meditation.

Take the standard posture of breathing with your hands over you abdomen. Then step out with one foot at 45 degrees and the other straight. Slowly shift your weight, as you gently rock back and forth. Slowly feel the weight distribution going to your front leg and then to your back leg. Try to get into a gentle see-saw kind of meditative movement, moving back and forth. Notice all the feelings and emotions within your body. Focus on relaxing as you gently move back and forth; you are trying to flow with the movement.

You can even do this form by walking across the length of the entire room. It's a great walking meditation, if you have the space.

OTHER SIDE

Exercise 4: *Eagle Stance.*

This form is about reaching out and relaxing all the extremities of your body, including your wrist, ankle, shoulder, fingers, and toes. This form should be done once on each side to balance out your body.

Begin by turning your foot on a 45 degree angle, and, from there, shift your weight to your back foot. Keep an 80% to 20% weight distribution when starting out, with eyes slightly open or closed. As you move, you will slowly distribute your weight in an even and smooth way. As you inhale, open up, remembering to always relax; it's easy to tense your shoulders while doing this form, so focus on relaxing them.

Turn your focus inward, focusing on all the feelings and sensations within your body. With your hands placed over your stomach, use your tail bone to lean back; then, follow with a backwards scooping motion as you inhale. Circle your arms, shifting your weight forward to follow your movement. With both arms now in front, let one arm be a little lower with your palm matching at the opposite elbow. As you exhale, sink into the posture, relaxing your knees, hips, and ankle joints.

From there, come into a standing moving meditation posture. Inhale open, starting with your elbows, followed by your forearms, wrists, and shoulders. As you exhale, close, starting with your elbows, forearms, wrists, and shoulders. Do this meditation a total of five to ten times on each side.

To shift to the other side, turn your leading foot in and use the other foot to step out 45 degrees. Then follow the same sequence as above.

OTHER SIDE

Exercise 5: *Frog Stance.* This is another great form for relaxing your spine, neck, and shoulders.

Begin doing diaphragmatic breathing: placing your hands over your stomach, not touching your stomach but slightly hovering over the area. Keep your feet shoulder-width apart, relaxing your knees slightly, coming into a comfortable stance. Begin by rotating both of your wrists up and slowly guide your hands up beginning with your elbows, then forearms, then wrists.

Bring hands in front of your chest with your palms facing inward. From there, open with your arms on the inhale and slowly close in with your arms on the exhale. Do this a total of 5 to 10 times. From there, slowly lower your arms back to hover over the stomach area.

MEDITATION MUSCLE THROUGH PRACTICE

The mindfulness practices and meditation moves I have shown you in this chapter will help you to build up your "meditation muscle" in order to access more positive states of mind. In my opinion, it's in your prefrontal cortex and your mind's energy field, both inside and outside of your body, that you have free will to choose and act. Great athletes know about the mind's energy field. For a basketball player, that field is both in the ball and part of the entire court. In football, when a quarterback is scrambling in the pocket and his receiver is in the end zone, he's aware that his mind field also extends to the receiver.

I hope that, through meditation, you become more conscious of this energetic mind field and work to strengthen it in your meditation practice and in everything you do. You can use your "meditation muscle" in order to have greater control of the push and pulls coming from the animal side of your brain. Your animal brain is powerful and full of desires, drives, and impulses. Although you can't control everything your animal brain does, you can use mindful attention to shift away from fears, desires, and pain. This is where the real meditation muscle takes place, giving you greater ability to focus your attention. The goal is strengthening your meditation muscle in a direct and specific ways through exercises I provide in my system.

CHAPTER 6

MEDITATION AND SUCCESS
IN BUSINESS AND SPORTS

Some of the most successful people in America meditate regularly. They do it for a host of reasons, from relieving stress and increasing well-being to gaining a clearer mind for optimal performance and efficiency. It's becoming more and more commonplace to see meditation and mindfulness practiced in corporate America, as well as in sports and many other endeavors.

MEDITATION IN CORPORATE AMERICA

Companies such as Google, Facebook, and Twitter all encourage meditation in the work place. Google actually has a separate room for senior staff to go and meditate whenever they feel like it. More and more American corporations are encouraging all employees to do regular meditation to reduce stress, increase productivity, and have an overall greater sense of well-being.

Here are a few superstars of this promising trend:

Ray Dalio, a prominent hedge fund manager, and founder and CEO of Bridgewater Associates, practices Transcendental Meditation, a form that relies on repeating a mantra while sitting. Dalio, worth an estimated $12.9 billion, uses meditation because he says it makes him more creative. He also claims meditation helps him stay centered throughout the day and avoid episodes of emotional hijacking.

Promega Corp., a biotech company that employs around 1,200 people internationally and has over $300 million in revenue, offers meditation and yoga to its employees. Promega is one of several companies all over the world offering mindfulness activities to reduce stress and sharpen focus. Companies are losing increasing numbers of people to sick days because of stress and exhaustion, so meditation is seen as a way to keep people at work.

General Mills, a Fortune 500 company, has been a major player in introducing mindfulness into the workplace.

Mark Bertolini, CEO of Aetna, is a huge advocate of meditation practice in the workplace. He broke his neck in a skiing accident and suffered such severe pain that he went on a mission to find some kind of non-drug relief. In this search, he came upon yoga and meditation, and liked the practice so much that he introduced it to his employees at Aetna. Since then, Bertolini has seen a 69-minute gain in productivity of employees over a year, and he thinks the meditation and yoga program played a role in the gain. The company has around 30,000 employees that insure 17 million people. A study done by Duke University School of Medicine with Atena employees concluded that yoga and meditation had dramatically reduced stress.

William George, a board member of the financial firm Goldman Sachs and former CEO of Medtronic, has been an advocate for bringing meditation into corporations since 1974.

The list is growing, now including CEO Jeff Weiner of LinkedIn, co-founder of Twitter and Square Jack Dorsey, Panda Express founder Andrew Cherng, co-founder of Sandbox Industries Bob Shapiro, CEO Roger Berkowitz of Legal Sea Foods, CEO Rick Goings of Tupperware, and former Chairman and CEO Ramani Ayer of The Hartford Financial. An event called "Wisdom 2.0 Business," founded by Soren Gordhamer, brings together some of the top leaders in business to discuss introduce more mindful practices into the workplace.

JOURNALIST WHO MEDITATE

Arianna Huffington, a cultural icon of journalism and business, literally pioneered blogging and put it on the map. *Time* said she is one of the most influential women in the world. Her online newspaper, *The Huffington Post,* is one of the most trusted new sources in all of journalism. Its international spread reaches to almost every country in the world.

Huffington is now on a mission to make the world more focused on well-being, mindfulness, empathy, and giving back. In her new book, *The Third Metric to Redefining Success and Creating a Life of Well-Being, Wisdom, and Wonder,* she explains how she radically changed her life after she was sitting at her desk one day and literally passed out from exhaustion. She hit her face on her desk, breaking her cheekbone and cutting the skin over her eye. At the time, she was 100 percent focused on her work and hadn't been getting enough sleep.

George Stephanopoulos, the host of *Good Morning America,* does meditation every day because it helps him stay focused throughout the day and helps him sleep better. When talking with Arianna Huffington at a Third Metric event, he said, "It's been a lifesaver for me." George is Greek Orthodox, and he did not approach the practice as a religious or spiritual practice. He came to the practice because his friends told him about all the scientific benefits of doing meditation, and he wanted some of them for himself.

Dan Harris, co-anchor of the weekend edition of *Good Morning America* and anchor of *Nightline,* details in his book, *10% Happier: How I Tamed the Voice in My Head, Reduced Stress*

Without Losing My Edge, and Found Self-Help That Actually Works, how he had a panic attack live on air, and then learned to meditate.

MEDITATION FOR ATHLETES

As anyone who has ever played a sport knows that the biggest opponent is always your own mind. Meditation gives you ways to come to terms with this opponent. Every athlete knows that what separates champions from non-champions is the mental game. The difference between a professional and amateur is how the athlete uses his or her mind.

The champions in all areas of sports are those who can pull strength from places where it doesn't seem humanly possible. This happens in the mind. It doesn't matter what sport you play—you can benefit from the positive benefits of meditation. Meditation research on athletic performance is still very much in its infancy, but if I were a player, I wouldn't wait for the research. In ten years, everybody is going to be meditating before the game. One of the biggest problems athletes face is the regulation of their stress and heart beat rate. Just the right amount of stress puts them in "the zone," while too much of it has a basketball player throwing bricks at the rim.

Every professional coach in the world should be looking at the thousands of studies that have shown the effectiveness of meditation. Phil Jackson, one of the all-time winning coaches in the NBA with 11 NBA championships, has been using meditation for years with his players.

RE-FOCUSING AND RESILIENCE

We are all amazed how some of the greatest athletes in the world are able to re-focus their attention and turn around results in their game. There's a famous story of Michael Jordan waking up in his hotel room during the NBA finals, feeling like he was about to die. It's the middle of the finals against the Utah Jazz, and the series is tied 2 to 2. Jordan, one the leading scorers on the Chicago Bulls, thought he might have been poisoned. As he lay in his bed, he called in the Bulls' medical professionals, who concluded he either had a stomach virus or food poisoning. It was an off day for the Bulls, so Jordan had to miss practice that day.

The day of the game, Jordan musters up the energy to pull himself out of bed and get to the Delta Center to face the Utah Jazz. Arriving early, he finds a dark room near the Bulls' locker room where he lies down, closes his eyes, and starts to visualize playing in the game at peak condition. A few minutes later, he opens his eyes and tells Coach Jackson that he's ready to play.

In the first quarter, Jordan can do absolutely nothing—he's hurting, and hurting bad. Some think he might not be able to continue, but he keeps pressing on. By the second quarter, Utah takes a 16 point lead, and something inside fuels Jordan to come back. He's able to shift his focus away from the pain in his body towards winning the game, and he ends up dominating that quarter by scoring 17 points. At halftime, Jordan rehydrates himself and tries to regain his health. In the third quarter, he gets hit again by the pain, which drags him down. In the fourth, he comes back again and makes several game-clinching points. The Bulls ended up winning that game, 90-87.

The question is how can a person have so much go wrong physically and still continue to press on? What makes a human being that resilient?

Martin Paulus, a researcher at the University of California at San Diego, is looking for ways the average person can develop professional level resilience and agility—like that of Michael Jordan. Together with his team, he's looking at how to train the brain to be more resilient by comparing the brains of ultra-resilient individuals with the general population, and finding how to train the general population to become more resilient.

The areas of the brain the researchers are examining include the *insular cortex* and the *medial prefrontal cortex*. The insular cortex is involved in self-awareness, cognitive functioning, motor control, and perception. The medial prefrontal cortex takes the role of the manager in responding to the emotions and perceptions from the insular cortex. Paulus looked at the brains of three groups of subjects—Marines, high-performance athletes (adventure racers), and average people—in fMRI brain scanning machines after putting them through cognitive tasks that made them highly stressed. Then the researchers further added to the stress by restricting all subjects' breathing, telling them in advance that the breathing restriction was coming. The Marines and high-performance athletes did the best on the cognitive task, of all three groups. They had a higher level of activation in their insular cortex before the restricted breathing test was administered, meaning they anticipated it and so were more prepared.

This might be why an athlete like Michael Jordan can be so resilient—he's been dealing with stress and setbacks for almost his entire life, dealing with situations over and over again in the past where he had to be resilient.

Such resilience, Paulus proposed, is possible through training in meditation. He put 30 Marine recruits through a mindfulness course to teach them non-judgmental awareness. The study found after an 8-week course that the recruits developed brain activity similar to the Marines and high-performance athletes in the earlier study, and this brain change lasted an entire year. Conclusion? Meditation is way for the average person to build resiliency and be able to shift focus when obstacles and stress seem overwhelming.

TOP EIGHT BENEFITS FOR ATHLETES

Here are ten top benefits of meditation for athletes or anyone who plays a sport.

1. *Meditation may help you focus.* Your focus will determine if you win or lose a game. Why not train your mind to focus? A study in the journal *Psychological Science* done at University of California, Davis suggested that meditation increases states of focus within the brain. Every athlete, no matter what sport they are playing, could work on improving their focus.

2. *Meditation may help you cope with pain.* There's an old cliché around professional athletes that, no matter what, they are always dealing with some kind of pain. High endurance sports do a number on your body. Researchers at Wake Forest University School of Medicine showed in a study that meditation helped with pain.

3. *Meditation may help you deal with fear.* Fear can hijack your mind from the present moment, leading to many errors. A study published in the *Frontiers in Human Neuroscience* done at Massachusetts General Hospital, Boston University, Emory University, University of Arizona, and Santa Barbara institute for Consciousness Studies showed that meditation helped calm the fear center of the brain, even when you're not meditating.

4. *Meditation strengthens your immune system.* An athlete cannot afford to be sick; if you're sick you can't play. Athletes are always looking at various ways to avoid becoming sick, so why not trying meditation? A study published in the journal *Perspectives on Psychological Science* done at Harvard University and Justus Liebig-University showed that meditation could strengthen the immune system.

5. *Meditation could make you resilient.* The greatest athletes in the world are the most resilient, and meditation has been shown to help out in this area. Everyone knows you have to fail over and over again until you succeed. Meditation helps you detach yourself from the negative thoughts that keep

you from achieving your goals. A study by the University of Wisconsin at Madison suggested that meditation may make people more resilient.

6. ***Meditation may reduce mental stress.*** Athletes are always under stress. They pride themselves on the ability to be in a high-stress environment. Why not embrace a practice that has been shown to reduce stress? Incorporating a little bit of meditation before the game could help. A study published in *JAMA Internal Medicine* that was done at The Johns Hopkins University shows that it may reduce anxiety, depression, and pain.

7. ***Meditation may help to stabilize emotions.*** One study done by the University of Utah showed that people with more mindful traits are better able to stabilize their emotions and have better control over their moods. The competitive nature of all athletes causes them to have to deal with a roller coaster of different emotions. Why not embrace meditation and uses mindfulness throughout the game?

8. ***Meditation may help with sleep.*** One night of lost sleep could lose a championship; quality sleep is one of the most valuable things every athlete should have. A study presented at the American Academy of Sleep Medicine suggested that meditation may help with sleep.

Meditation could be that extra edge that helps you get the game-winning point or go the extra mile when you think you can't. Why not incorporate it into your training regime? It just might make you a better athlete.

HOW TO MEDITATE BEFORE A GAME

The first thing every high performance athlete knows is that he or she has to manage nervous energy. I've heard countless stories of athletes who felt like they were going to throw up before a game, especially when the stakes were high, as in a championship game.

Next time you are feeling anxious before participating in a sports event, follow these five steps to relax and have a better chance to succeed:

1. First, always remember that you are not the feelings in your body. You're not the fear, and you're not the nervous energy.
2. Separate from the anxious feeling by focusing on breathing in through your nose to your diaphragm. Remember, deep diaphragmatic breathing calms the nervous system.
3. Work on bringing up a positive memory, maybe a memory you had as a child.
4. Once you have the feeling from that memory, let it fill your entire body until you feel great.
5. Open your eyes. Try to focus on holding this feeling and come back to this state whenever you feel anxious.

CHAPTER 7
MEDITATION FOR STRESS REDUCTION

There's just no avoiding the stress of modern living. You can't escape it; it's here to stay. But with a regular meditation practice, you can survive stress, and even thrive in today's high-stress environment at work, in your family, and even riding along the super highways of today's high-speed travel.

We all pay the toll of not being able to deal well with stress. Stress is the number one cause of toxic emotions. If not managed, stress can derail your career, ruin your love life, and compromise your brainpower. It saps your energy, causes you to do irrational things, and even makes you stupid. To do away with these feelings that result from stress, you do all kinds of irrational behaviors, such as eat an obscene amount of junk food or swear at your friends, spouse, and coworkers.

Most of this stress comes from the annoying chatter in your mind that is filled with worries, doubts, fears, and other nonsense. What most people are searching for when they indulge in irrational behaviors is a feeling—they want a quick-fix good feeling. Like the occasional indulgence of your favorite junk food, there's nothing wrong with this. However, a problem arises when these behaviors become addictions.

Instead of engaging in these negative behaviors, you can use two of the greatest tools in the world to reduce stress—meditation and laughter. Both of these activities open your mind, clear away stressful feelings, and help you engage with people more effectively.

BENEFITS OF LAUGHTER

Some evolutionary psychologists argue that laughter existed even before we learned how to speak. One could make the argument that laughter is a survival mechanism that has helped keep our species alive for tens of thousands of years. This may be true for several reasons. First, laughter is a major stress reliever; when you laugh, you dampen the stress hormones in your body that are causing havoc. Second, laughter is a way to bond with another human being and remove fear in a conversation. Imagine you are a caveman walking in the desert. All of the sudden, you see a stranger approaching you with a large club. As the stranger gets closer, you get more afraid, until one of you cracks a joke and you both start laughing. Immediately, you form a social bond with each other from this strong experience. You went from being fearful to laughing.

Laughter can bring about the most nourishing emotions in your life, making things better for everyone. Every subculture has a way to deal with hardships through laughter; even people in high-stress occupations, like paramedics, will find ways to incorporate laughter into their work. They are better at dealing with horrific accidents because laughter helps to relieve some of the emotional impact that goes along with the job.

Meditation is a tool to become more conscious of the feeling of joy and laughter that is always within us. Once we come to know such exhilaration, we can learn to utilize it in our relationships throughout the day. Why not practice cultivating laughter and joy every day through meditation?

Meditation can essentially be seen as emotional weight-lifting for the mind. If we do meditation in the morning and focus on the feeling of laughter, then we can carry that feeling with us throughout the day. However, a lot of people say that, when they meditate, they feel an incredible sense of deep calm and happiness, but then they go through a stressful day at the workplace and lose it all.

If we learn to hold onto the feeling of laughter inside our body, then we can interpret the world in a more fulfilling and stress-free way. What if you were to carry that same attitude of humor throughout your entire day? Can you imagine how much it would improve your day? What if you went to work every day with the attitude, *I wish for everyone I meet today to find humor in their lives?*

This type of training could be incorporated throughout your entire day. If you find yourself stressed in the middle of the day, try to bring your attention back to your breathing, and work on bringing feelings of laughter and joyful humor to the surface. Here's how:

LAUGHTER MEDITATION

1. Find a comfortable place to sit. Bring your attention to your breathing; watch your breath as you slowly breathe in and out.
2. Bring your attention to your belly; breathe as if your belly is filling up with water. As you breathe, let go of any tension that you may have in your body.
3. Now bring up an image of something you find very funny. Then once you have that feeling, try to spread it throughout your entire body.
4. Then bring up another image of something you find to be hilarious. Again, work on spreading that feeling throughout your entire body.
5. Keep breathing and working on noticing the feeling of laughter inside your body. This simple meditation will help you to carry this feeling throughout your day. It will reduce stress, build strong relationships, and give you a greater sense of well-being.

STRESS AND YOUR EMOTIONS

For thousands of years, Eastern traditions have recognized how the mind goes from extreme states of joy to extreme states of sadness and worry. Monks from Eastern traditions were essentially scientists; they recognized that such a wild mind could adversely affect health. They developed meditation as a way to stay in emotional balance throughout the day.

It's a no-brainer that stress is extremely damaging to our health. The goal of meditation is not only to monitor your breathing, but also to monitor your emotions. In Traditional Chinese medicine, the first thing you are told about disease prevention is to monitor your emotions, because negative feelings cause your body to become unbalanced, leading to a variety of health problems.

In traditional Eastern health care systems, doctors would do a few minutes of meditation before they saw a patient, so they could have a clear mind. This is something we should incorporate into our American workplaces. Burnout is a major problem in the work place, and one of the most stressed demographics of society is medical doctors. Physicians have to deal with a whole host of various stressors. A study reported in the *Journal of the American Medical Association*, done at the University of Rochester showed that doctors who used mindfulness practices had lower levels of burnout than people who do not practice mindfulness. In addition, the mindfulness practices they did showed long-lasting effects up to a year later.

My family doctor, Dr. Lin, whom I've known since I was 12, always did meditation before seeing his patients. The hallways of his office were filled with pictures of patients and family members of patients. Many of his patients were very sick children coming to him as their last hope, and he helped them to recover through various natural health approaches. Dr. Lin hugely impacted my life, as his compassion towards people was second to none. He was the first person to introduce me to meditation and mindfulness. This man practiced mindful awareness with all of his patients.

And he knew the power of laughter and humor. Dr. Lin handed out smiley faces stickers to everyone: children and adults. I think this attitude itself is healing. Imagine if every doctor made his/her patients smile when they left.

STRESS AND WORK

Business in America and in the world in large is about delivering value to the marketplace. A major part of this equation for success is customer service, because if the employees of a company don't treat people well, it can dramatically affect profits. Unfortunately, many employees in America are stressed out and unable to provide valuable service.

When an employee is stressed out, he or she is going to make poor decisions and have a bad attitude towards customers. A survey done by the American Psychological Association found that one-third of employees experience chronic stress related to work. Meditation is a tool that could be used to address this problem in the workplace. Oprah has all of her employees at Harpo Studios doing Transcendental Meditation.

Meditation can help you to be present in your workplace, and to look at a task and complete it with a clear mind. When you are stressed, your focus is all over the place. Every CEO in America should be encouraging employees to find some solitude and quiet time. If employees are taught how to manage emotions that are magnified by stress, less burnout will ensue.

EMOTIONAL CONTROL AND STRESS

Let's face it, most of us have a constant daily battle with emotions and in response, do all types of things to satisfy cravings from over-eating to using illegal drugs. We all deal with our minds' obsessive thoughts and feelings that bombard us daily. The goal is to get the mind to stop engaging with these thoughts and feelings that put us at the risk of stress-related illness and wreak havoc in our relationships.

A steady mindfulness practice helps you to build space that can buffer you from your wild emotional mind. You can become an expert at training your mind if you really work at it. It's something you have to dedicate a lot of effort to perfecting, but it's totally worth it.

Remember: *You are not your thoughts or emotions.*

At this time, scientists can't explain exactly what the mind actually is. For thousands of years, Eastern traditions have talked about the idea of "no self." If you think about it, the self is what causes all the problems. There's an old American cowboy proverb that says, *The biggest troublemaker you'll probably ever have to deal with watches you shave his face in the mirror every morning.*

Mindfulness throughout the day gives you the ability to understand and observe your own ego. This single practice is immensely gratifying and can help you to recognize the true guiding force in your life. Meditation will help you to remove the road blocks that are in your way. If you are not getting the results you want, it's because of how you are internalizing things too much. Meditation helps you to enter into the flow state where ideas and solutions are abundant, and where you can just be.

STRESS AND ADDICTION

Stress can make you do some silly things, like binge eat an entire bag of potato chips. This is because, when you are under stress, the reward center of your brain is looking for a temporary fix. Researchers showed this phenomenon with rats in the lab; when shocked unpredictably, the rats make a run for a quick fix, seeking drugs, alcohol, sugar, or whatever reward stimulus is presented. Anyone who has smoked and tried to quit can be heard saying, *I just can't right now, I'm too stressed.* Or maybe they've tried and then relapsed when under extreme stress.

There are many mindfulness programs available for alcoholics and drug addicts. Dr. Judson Brewer at the Yale School Medicine studies mindfulness and addictions and has used mindfulness techniques to help people overcome various addictions such as smoking, drugs, and alcohol. His evidence-based program, also available as an app to help people quit smoking, can be found at www.cravingtoquit.com.

Many addictions occur because we believe that drugs, alcohol, or whatever will temporarily relieve stress. And they do—temporarily. However, the problem is that, every time we engage in that behavior, we reinforce the circuits associated with the addiction. The brain doesn't care; it simply deals with the input that you're giving it. Whether you make bad choices or good choices, your brain goes down the same road. Binge eaters suffer from this problem every time they become stressed and immediately turn to food. Each time they do this, they are making that connection stronger and stronger, reinforcing the brain's neural networks.

The only way to break from an addiction is to decide that you are going to change. You have to become mindful of the process that leads to addiction; once you are mindful of it, you can start to get space from the feelings that drive the addiction. When you get space from those feelings, you can change the behavior of addiction.

FOUR WAYS MEDITATION CAN HELP TO REDUCE STRESS

Here are four ways to use meditation to reduce stress:

1. *Go out into nature.* Go out for a walk in nature. You can do walking meditation with your eyes open by just bringing your attention to your breathing. Meditating in nature will help you realign with your body.
2. *Meditate in the morning to prevent stress.* You can prevent a lot of future stress responses throughout your day by doing meditation right when you wake up. Make a commitment to do five to ten minutes of meditation every morning. You will have a lot less stress in your life.
3. *Be aware of the stress feelings in your body.* Most of your day-to-day activities move your attention away from the feelings in your body. Learn to recognize when you are getting stressed out. When you feel you are getting stressed, stop what you are doing and do some meditation.
4. *Do meditation during your lunch break.* If you do five to fifteen minutes of meditation during your lunch break every day, you will see almost immediate results. Set a reminder on your calendar or in your phone to stop and do meditation right before you eat lunch.

PUT YOUR CELL PHONE ASIDE

A recent Internet trends report by Kleiner, Perkins, Caufield, & Byers suggested that the average person checks his or her smartphone 150 times a day. I see this problem as one of the biggest plagues in our society since the bubonic plague.

The only difference between the cell phone plague and the bubonic plague is that the bubonic plague showed physical symptoms of its effects, like coughing, bleeding, and vomiting. Most people addicted to their cell phones aren't even conscious of what they're doing to their lives, especially to their loved ones, friends, and children, or the people they are putting in harm's way by driving while using their cell phone. According to the National Safety Council, 28 percent of car accidents occur from people talking or text messaging on their cell phones. At least 200,000 car accidents have been caused by texting while driving. There's even a term for cell phone addiction called *nomophobia,* meaning "no-mobile-phone phobia."

For thousands of years, we operated socially by having intimate conversations with each other in which we laughed, told stories, and connected face to face. Today, people are glued to their cells phones when they could be interacting with others. I was at a café recently and saw five teenagers sitting on a couch, all glued to their cell phones and not talking to each other for an entire hour. When they got up to leave, I noticed one of them, still glued to his smartphone, had left his bag behind. To get his attention, I had to yell so loud across the room that I disrupted half the people in the café to tell this young man that he'd forgotten his bag. He ran back, picked up his bag, saying, "Thanks, man!" and rushed off.

Moreover, too much cell phone use may be linked to depression in teens. One survey done by the Pew Institute suggested that Americans in the age range of 18 to 29 years old send 88 text messages a day. Another study suggested that too much stimulus from multiple electronic devices may be linked to depression and anxiety.

There is a better place to cultivate positive emotions that will make us happier and more fulfilled. Those emotions are within us, and, by blocking these feelings with all of our latest technologies, we may be harming ourselves.

We need to take back control of our minds and stop compulsively checking our emails, Facebook updates, and text messages. I think we can live happier and more compassionate lives if we tune into ourselves and the people we are speaking with. How many relationships are lost because of a lack of communication? Think about what a parent is doing to a child's emotional well-being when Mom or Dad is focused on a cell phone rather than on a child's needs. The goal of enjoying life is to be here now, to live a life full of wonder and astonishment. That way we can truly experience all of what life has to offer.

The goal of mindfulness is to be in the moment, instead of letting your mind ruminate or compulsively check your cell phone. Work on training your focus on what you're doing—if you're eating just eat, try to taste everything. If you are playing with your child at the park, be totally attentive to what he or she is doing. If you are in a business meeting and someone is speaking, listen to everything the person has to say. Cell phones and other technologies are here to stay; it's not the technology—it's the user that is the problem. Just remember: *Your cell phone is not part of your body.*

TAKE A BREAK FROM YOUR CELL

Put limits on your cell phone use, especially if you have children. Remember, children are delicate and sensitive, and their brains need proper nourishment in order to grow. If you ignore your children and pay attention to your cell phone instead, it's going to cause problems in the future.

Moreover, you don't need the depression and anxiety in your life caused from too much cell phone use. Here are some rules to follow to prevent over-use of your cell:

Rule #1: Don't sleep next to your cell phone. Put it in the kitchen.

Rule #2: Put your cell phone away when you get home from work.

Rule #3. Don't check your cell phone first thing when you wake up. Go to the bathroom, drink water, or eat first.

FEAR AND STRESS

Fear is an immensely powerful emotion. Your brain is capable of causing a tsunami of fear chemicals that flood your body and cause you do irrational things. People under extreme stress have problems dialing 911 because, in the grip of fear, their fine motor skills go right out the window. Even law enforcement and military professionals can lose bladder control during a gun fight with a criminal. This not their fault; rather, it is an automatic response by the body during extreme fear. When the body is preparing to fight or flee, it doesn't care about bladder control. Scuba divers have been known to die in the ocean after pulling the regulator out of their mouth in a panic; they died with a full tank of air. Their "old brain" activates and says, "need air now!" So they panic, pull the regulator out and try to get as much air in their mouth as possible. There are also instances of policemen trying to fire a gun with the safety still on, repeatedly pulling the trigger even though nothing is happening.

When evolution designed the brain, it didn't take into consideration gun safety locks or air regulators. Rather, it was designed more to survive when an animal like a bear attacks: you either run or continue to punch the bear until it lets go. These are automatic, unconscious processes of the old brain. It may have not been the best method, but it worked for a large number of people, in order for the genes to be passed on. When your body gets in this condition, it's called *Condition Black*. Your mind will perform the same task over and over again, regardless of the results. The government spends a tremendous amount of money each year to study fear and stress in order to help military officials and law enforcement respond well in emergencies. The one factor they study the most is heart rates of people operating in high-stress environments.

Lt. Col. Dave Grossman and Loren W. Christensen, in their book *On Combat: The Psychology and Physiology of Deadly Conflict in War and in Peace,* point to a study done on U. S. Army Special Forces to test heart rate variability, using some of the most elite military personal in the best physical condition possible. They carried out a "stress test" where Special Forces operatives had to partake in a course with hand-to-hand combat, electrical shots (simulating gunshots), full equipment, and paint bullet guns. This took place in a poorly lit environment with loud noises to purposely offset them. The soldiers performed incredibly under this stress, the best at about 175 bpm, just on the brink of Condition Black. To give you an idea, Condition White is a normal resting heart rate at 60 to 80 bpm.

In that same course, a stress study was done to see if Green Berets could handcuff a person when the Berets' heart rate is in that same high range of Condition Grey (140 to 180 bpm). They used what are called "flex cuffs" that look like thin, plastic durable strips. A high level of motor control is needed to get the straps through a loop, similar to threading a shoestring through the lace holes of a shoe.

At the time, this training was not thoroughly engrained into the Green Berets' muscle memory; they had not trained for it yet. Because of this, many of them had a tough time handcuffing their subjects. However, when they had "pre-threaded" their handcuffs before putting them on, it was done very easily.

So what does this tell us? It shows that even the most trained military professionals in the world lose fine motor skill under stress, and so the average person can be expected to lose them a whole lot easier. That's why people forget how to dial 911 when under extreme pressure. The rational, logical part of the brain thinks you are capable of dialing 911, but under extreme stress your more primitive amygdala hijacks your frontal lobes, causing you to act more like a gorilla than a human. You can see physical changes in people who go into Condition Black—their face turns white and they sometimes pass out. Some people go into Condition Black when they are getting their blood drawn at a hospital, passing out from the stress and fear accompanied by a severely elevated heart rate. Furthermore, when in Condition Black, you don't think clearly because you're dealing with a disorienting adrenalin dump.

STRESS RESPONSE AND PERFORMANCE

There are several programs currently being used in the military to help soldiers reduce stress. One of them is Mindfulness-Based Mind Fitness Training (MMFT). MMFT is a class that is taught over an eight-week period, designed for people working in stressful environments. The program teaches stress resilience skills and mindfulness skills, giving specific exercises to build attention control and concentration. Another program, the Samueli Institute's Center for Military Medical Research, teaches various complementary and integrative health care practices to be used at military medical centers, veteran's hospitals, and in other military settings.

Some of the greatest research on stress and performance has come from studies done on the American military's Special Forces units. Our Special Forces go through the most demanding physical and mental training in the world.

Dr. Andy Morgan at Yale Medical School is one of the researchers on the topic of stress in the military. In one of the trainings, his team put Special Forces trainers under mock interrogations, during which their heart rate went up to 170 beats a minute for over a period of a half hour. When heart rate gets over 175 beats per minute, several things start happening to your body. Tunnel vision sets in, you're vulnerable to loss of bladder control, and fine motor skills diminish.

The trainees in this study lost an average of 22 pounds in three days from such stressful training. Researchers measured *norepinephrine* in the body to measure how the soldiers were coping with stress. Norepinephrine is one of many chemicals used by the brain to keep frontal lobes in check for critical thinking. The best way to build up stress tolerance is by training in high stress environments.

At a very fundamental level, one of the ways to slow the heart rate down is deep breathing. Controlled deep breathing helps to send signals to the sympathetic nervous system to slow down the overactive heart. This is one of the reasons why the military is using meditation as a tool for soldiers to combat stress.

Athletes also make use of this practice. What's one of the first things a professional basketball player does before a free throw? He takes several deep breaths. Many boxers and mixed martial artists also monitor their heart rate before they go out into the ring or cage. When they walk out, they're taking deep breaths to slow their heart rate down.

Focusing your attention on your breathing has been shown to help stop excessive mental rumination. A mind ruminating is a mind out of control. When you have 30 seconds left in a basketball game, and your team is down by a point, the last thing you want is a mind that is all over the place. You have more important things to worry about—like winning the game.

Why not become a professional yourself at controlling breathing? What's the easiest way to do this? Meditation. The Samurai and other warrior cultures have been using meditation for thousands of years to train their focus and be effective in battle. These cultures knew one thing very well: fear is an emotion that derails attention, and an unfocused state of mind is not good for survival.

CURB YOUR STRESS RESPONSE (AND SAVE YOUR LIFE ONE DAY)

If you ever find yourself in a situation where your stress level has elevated considerably, pause for a moment and take five deep breaths from your belly. The first rule to curb a stress response is to focus on your breathing. By taking slow, rhythmic, deep breaths you are activating the area of your brain known as the pre-frontal cortex and slowing down the activity in your amygdala.

You are also controlling heart rate variability, and people with higher heart rate variability are better at self-control. Meditation and physical exercise are two of the best ways to increase baseline heart variability, and they both also strengthen the prefrontal cortex.

If you meditate and do physical exercise every day, you will not only improve the quality of your health, but, when you encounter a stressful situation, you will be prepared for a possible emergency, as well.

THE CHATTER IN YOUR HEAD

It's just human—we all have that little voice in our head. This voice says a lot of nonsense, like you're not good enough to start a business, you're too fat to wear those jeans, you're not good enough to get into grad school. Most of this chatter comes from things we hear in our peer groups, things people told us as children, etc. This chatter gets worse when you are under stress and fear, and it's at those times you react emotionally and do things you wouldn't normally do, such as yell at your co-workers or swear at your spouse.

But in reality, that stress-induced chatter in your head is *not you*. For thousands of years, Eastern traditions have been going to war against that chatter with a most effective weapon—meditation. Much of the anxiety we experience is the result of self-focusing, meaning when you think excessively about what's going on in your own body and mind. Sometimes just shifting your focus away from yourself and onto helping others can quell that anxiety. Compassion is one of the greatest gifts you can offer to another human being. It's something we all need biologically.

As we get older, we tend to become closed, having been through a series of setbacks which include failed relationships and other failures. The voice in your head sometimes replays those failures over and over again. But that movie tape playing in your head is not you! It changes constantly, depending on how you feel.

Mark Twain said it best: "The best way to cheer yourself up is to try to cheer somebody else up." Science now proves this age-old wisdom. Compassion works.

If you walked out your house every morning and said, "Today I'm going to make another person happy," it would cause a ripple effect to go out to many other people in the world. A psychologist named James H. Fowler looked at data of 5,000 people in a period of over 20 years. He found that happiness radiated out to influence people through three degrees, meaning friends of friends of friends, and it lasted an entire year.

Happiness is contagious, and it's capable of spreading like wildfire. Remember that you are literally changing the world by having a positive upbeat attitude. You might not be noticing it, but it's true. By walking through your life in a happy compassionate state, you are spreading happiness wherever you go.

Here are a few parting suggestions for maintaining that positive attitude through mindful awareness:

KEEP A POSITIVE THROUGH MINDFUL AWARENESS

1. *Be grateful:* Throughout your day, simply stop what you're doing and just look up at the sky. Be thankful to be alive. Be thankful for all the people in your life.
2. *Laugh:* Think about a time when you had a good laugh and feel flood of laughter in every area of your body.
3. *Forgive:* Forgive people who have wronged you in your life. Be mindful of letting negative feelings towards them go and feel the freedom that results.
4. *Care about others:* Compassion works and giving to others makes you happy.

I hope that one day, I can walk into a gym, or corporate boardroom and see people meditating. I hope that the surgeon general's office recommends people to do daily meditation to receive all the health benefits it has to offer. I think America would be better as whole if everyone really decided to turn inward, meditate, and reflect on what's going in the world.

I look forward to the day when everyone, no matter what religion they practice, sees meditation as a tool to improve the quality of his or her life. I recommend that you take as much as you can from this book and apply it to your daily life. Even if you only start with doing two minutes of meditation a day,

I recommend that you set some time up every day to do a little bit of meditation. It takes conscious effort to become good at meditation: it's not easy, but it's worth the effort.

As I stated previously, America is one of the most resilient countries in the world; the DNA of this country is made up of people who took risks and came from all over the world. I think Americans need to adopt a practice that's been shown to increase resilience and compassion. Cheers to America's new workout for the mind!

ABOUT THE AUTHOR

Robert Piper is a speaker, writer, Tai Chi master, and meditation teacher. He was first introduced to meditation by a board certified physician with dual medical training (Western medicine and Traditional Chinese medicine) who later referred him to Taoist monk. He studied with the Taoist monk for nine and a half years, and traveled extensively to Asia and Australia searching out and studying with other teachers. He has spent over a decade researching, studying, and collecting information on various meditation systems of Asia. He's taught meditation at Walgreens University, John H. Stroger, Jr. Hospital of Cook County, and Mental Health America of Illinois. Robert has a BA degree from DePaul University and lives in Chicago, IL. He writes for *Origin Magazine, Huffington Post, Elephant Journal,* and *MindBodyGreen.* You can find more about Robert at his website, robertpiper.org.

Bibliography

Battis, Lila. "The Price of Pessimism." Men's Health. January/February, 2014.

Black, Harvey. "Meditate That Cold Away: Practicing meditation or exercising might make you sick less often." Scientific American. Oct 18, 2012. http://www.scientificamerican.com/article/meditate-that-cold-away/

Brookes, David. *The Social Animal: The Hidden Sources of Love, Character, and Achievement.* New York: Random House, 2011.

Cloud, John. "Losing Focus? Studies Say Meditation May Help." Time. August 6, 2010. http://content.time.com/time/health/article/0,8599,2008914,00.html

Csikszentmihalyi, M. *Flow: The Psychology of Optimal Experience.* New York: Harper Perennial Modern Classics, 2008.

D'amasio, Antonio. *Descartes' Error: Emotion, Reason, and the Human Brain.* New York: Penguin Books, 2005.

David DeSteno. "The Morality of Meditation." The New York Times, July 5, 2013. http://www.nytimes.com/2013/07/07/opinion/sunday/the-morality-of-meditation.html

Desbordes, Gaëlle, Lobsang T., Negi, Thaddeus W. W., Pace, B. Alan, Wallace, Raison, Charles L., and L. Schwartz, Eric. "Effects of mindful-attention and compassion meditation training on amygdala response to emotional stimuli in an ordinary, non-meditative state." Frontiers of Human Neuroscience. November 2012.

Gelles, David "The mind business" FT Magazine. August 24, 2012.   www.ft.com/cms/s/2/d9cb7940-ebea-11e1-985a-00144feab49a.html

Gonzales, Laurence. *Deep Survival: Who Lives, Who Dies, and Why.* New York: W. W. Norton, 2003.

———. *Surviving Survival: The Art and Science of Resilience.* New York: W. W. Norton, 2013.

Goyal, Madhav, Singh, Sonal, Erica M. S., Sibinga, Gould, Neda F. Rowland-Seymour, Anastasia, Sharma, Ritu, Berger, Zackary, Sleicher, Dana, Maron, David D., Shihab, Hasan M., Ranasinghe, Padmini D., Shauna, Linn, Saha, Shonali, Bass, Eric B., Haythornthwaite, Jennifer A. "Meditation Programs for Psychological Stress and Well-being: A Systematic Review and Meta-analysis." JAMA Internal Medicine, 2014.

Gregoire, Carolyn. "The Daily Habit Of These Outrageously Successful People." July 5, 2013. http://www.huffington-post.com/2013/07/05/business-meditation-executives-meditate_n_3528731.html

———. "This Is The New Favorite Pastime Of The Business Elite (Hint: It's Not Golf)." The Huffington Post. September 18, 2013. http://www.huffingtonpost.com/2013/09/18/leaders-meditation_n_3916003.html

Grossman, Lt. Col. Dave and Christensen, Loren W. *On Combat, the Psychology and Physiology of Deadly Conflict in War and in Peace.* Illinois: Warrior Science Publications, 2008.

Harding, Anne. "In Pain? Try meditation." CNN Health/Health.com. April 5, 2011 http://www.cnn.com/2011/HEALTH/04/05/meditation.reduce.pain/index.html

Harris, Dan. *10% Happier: How I Tamed the Voice in My Head, Reduced Stress Without Losing My Edge, and Found Self-Help That Actually Works.* New York: It Books, 2014.

Huffington, Arianna. *The Third Metric To Redefining Success and Creating a Life of Well-Being, Wisdom, and Wonder.* New York: Harmony, 2014.

Hutchinson, Alex. "Self-Talk Boosts Endurance." Runner's World. October 25, 2013. http://www.runnersworld.com/running-tips/self-talk-boosts-endurance

Johnson-Laird, Philip. *Mental Models: Towards a Cognitive Science of Language, Inference, and Consciousness.* Massachusetts: Harvard University Press, 1983.

LaFee, Scott. "War and Peace (of Mind): Meditation training may help reduce stress disorders among U.S. military personnel." UC San Diego News Center. May 16, 2004. http://ucsdnews.ucsd.edu/pressrelease/war_and_peace_of_mind

Laskowski, Tara. "New Study Shows Meditating Before Lecture Leads to Better Grades." George Mason News. April 9, 2013. http://newsdesk.gmu.edu/2013/04/new-study-shows-meditating-before-lecture-leads-to-better-grades/

LeDoux, Joseph. *The Emotional Brain: The Mysterious Underpinnings of Emotional Life.* New York: Simon & Schuster, 1996.

————. *Synaptic Self: How Our Brains Become Who We Are.* New York: Penguin Books, 2003.

Lin, Judy. "Mindfulness reduces stress, promotes resilience." UCLA News Room. July 29, 2009. http://newsroom.ucla.edu/stories/using-mindfulness-to-reduce-stress-96966

Lockhart, Jhaneel and Hicken, Melanie "14 Executives Who Swear By Meditation." Business Insider, 2012. http://www.businessinsider.com/ceos-who-meditate-2012-5

Luders, Eileen, Kurth, Florian, Mayer, Emeran A., Toga, Arthur W., Narr, Katherine L., Gaser, Christian. "The Unique Brain Anatomy of Meditation Practitioners: Alterations in Cortical Gyrification. Frontiers in Human Neuroscience." 2012; 6.

Kabat-Zinn, Jon. *Wherever You Go, There You Are.* New York: Hyperion, 2005.

Kanani, Rahim. "Consider Yourself an Expert? Think Again." Forbes. June 22, 2012. http://www.forbes.com/sites/rahimkanani/2012/06/22/consider-yourself-an-expert-think-again/

Kaufman, Marc. "Meditation Gives Brain a Charge, Study Finds." The Washington Post. January 3, 2005. http://www.washingtonpost.com/wp-dyn/articles/A43006-2005Jan2.html

Kelley, Peter. "Mindful multitasking: Meditation first can calm stress, aid concentration." University of Washington. June 13, 2012. http://www.washington.edu/news/2012/06/13/mindful-multitasking-meditation-first-can-calm-stress-aid-concentration/

Martin, Judy. "Stress at Work is Bunk for Business." Forbes. August 2, 2012. http://www.forbes.com/sites/work-in-progress/2012/08/02/stress-at-work-is-bunk-for-business/

McGonigal, Kelly. *The Willpower Instinct: How Self-Control Works, Why It Matters, and What You Can Do to Get More of It*. New York: Avery, 2011.

Reynolds, Gretchen. "Get Up. Get Out. Don't Sit." New York Times. October 17, 2012. http://well.blogs.nytimes.com/2012/10/17/get-up-get-out-dont-sit/

Sapolsky, Robert. *Why Zebras Don't Get Ulcers. New York: Henry Holt and Company, 2004.*

Schwartz, Jeffrey M. *Dear Patrick: Life is Tough—Here's Some Good Advice*. New York: HarperCollins e-books, 2011.

Shenk, Joshua Wolf. *Lincoln's Melancholy: How Depression Challenged a President and Fuelled His Greatness*. Massachusetts: Mariner Books, 2006.

Sheridan, Sam. *The Disaster Diaries: One Man's Quest to Learn Everything Necessary to Survive the Apocalypse*. New York: Penguin Book, 2014.

Sherwood, Ben. "Ultimate Stress Test: Special Forces Training." Newsweek, March 13, 2010. http://www.newsweek.com/ultimate-stress-test-special-forces-training-82749

Stern, Joanna. "Cellphone Users Check Phones 150x/Day and Other Internet Fun Facts." ABC NEWS. May 29, 2013.

http://abcnews.go.com/blogs/technology/2013/05/cellphone-users-check-phones-150xday-and-other-internet-fun-facts/

Suttie, Jill. "Better Eating through Mindfulness." Greater Good The Science of a Meaningful Life. June 27, 2012. http://greatergood.berkeley.edu/article/item/better_eating_through_mindfulness

Taylor, Marygrace. "The All-Natural Depression And Anxiety Solution." http://www.prevention.com/mind-body/emotional-health/meditaton-improves-depression-and-anxiety

Visser, Susanna N., Danielson, Melissa L., Bitsko Rebecca H., Holbrook, Joseph R., Kogan, Michael D., Ghandour, Reem M., Ruth, Perou, Blumberg, Stephen J. "Trends in the Parent-Report of Health Care Provider-Diagnosed and Medicated Attention-Deficit/Hyperactivity Disorder: United States, 2003–2011" Journal of the American Academy of Child & Adolescent Psychiatry. January 2014.

Wehrwein, Peter "Astounding increase in antidepressant use by Americans" Harvard Health Blog. October 20, 2011. http://www.health.harvard.edu/blog/astounding-increase-in-antidepressant-use-by-americans-201110203624

Wilson, Timothy D. *Strangers to Ourselves: Discovering the Adaptive Unconscious.* Massachusetts: Belknap Press, 2004.

Wise, Jeff "When Panic Proves Deadly: The fatal psychology of cave-diving." Psychology today. December 8, 2010. http://www.psychologytoday.com/blog/extreme-fear/201012/when-panic-proves-deadly

American Academy of Sleep Medicine. "Meditation May Be An Effective Treatment For Insomnia." ScienceDaily. Science Daily, June 15, 2009. http://www.sciencedaily.com/releases/2009/06/090609072719.htm

American Psychological Association. "APA Survey Finds US Employers Unresponsive to Employee Needs." American

Psychological Association Press Releases. http://www.apa. org/news/press/releases/2013/03/employee-needs.aspx

Harvard Medical School. "Happiness Is 'Infectious' In Network Of Friends: Collective – Not Just Individual – Phenomenon." ScienceDaily. ScienceDaily, 5 December 2008. www.sciencedaily.com/releases/2008/12/081205094506.htm

Harvard Medical School. "Stress and the sensitive gut" Harvard Mental Health Letter. August, 2010. http://www.health. harvard.edu/special_health_reports/the_sensitive_gut

Mayo Clinic. "Positive thinking: Stop negative self-talk to reduce stress." http://www.mayoclinic.org/healthy-living/ stress-management/in-depth/positive-thinking/ art-20043950

The University of Utah. "Better Living through Mindfulness." The University of Utah News Center. March 07, 2013 http://unews.utah.edu/news_releases/better-living-through-mindfulness/

University of California-Davis. "Mindfulness from meditation associated with lower stress hormone" UC Davis News and Information. March 27, 2013. http://www.news.ucdavis. edu/search/news_detail.lasso?id=10538

University of Rochester. "Being Mindful Promotes Good Mental Health." University of Rochester Newscenter. April 1, 2003. http://www.rochester.edu/news/show.php? id=728

University of Rochester. "Mindful Meditation, Shared Dialogues Reduce Physician Burnout." University of Rochester Newscenter. September 22, 2009 http://www. urmc.rochester.edu/news/story/index.cfm?id=2623

University Of Wisconsin-Madison. "University Of Wisconsin Study Reports Sustained Changes In Brain And Immune Function After Meditation." ScienceDaily. ScienceDaily, 4 February 2003. Http://www.sciencedaily.com/releases/ 2003/02/030204074125.htm

16875342R00080

Made in the USA
Middletown, DE
23 December 2014